Praxis® Special Education: Core Knowledge and Applications 5354

How to Pass the Praxis® 5354 by using effective test prep, proven strategies, and relevant practice test questions.

By: Kathleen Jasper, Ed.D.

Kathleen Jasper LLC
Estero, FL 33928
www.kathleenjasper.com | info@KathleenJasper.com

Praxis® Special Education: Core Knowledge and Applications 5354: How to pass the Praxis® 5354 by using effective test prep, proven strategies, practice test questions.

Printed in the United States of America
ISBN: 9798747841468

Kathleen Jasper

Thank you for taking the time to purchase this book. I really appreciate it.

Would you mind leaving a review?

Did you purchase this book on Amazon? If so, I would be thrilled if you would leave an unbiased review at your convenience. Did you purchase this book from KathleenJasper.com? If so, you can leave a review on Facebook, Google, or directly on our website on the product page. Thank you for using my products.

Visit my Facebook Page.

I post videos, practice test questions, upcoming events, and other resources daily on my Facebook Page. Join us every Tuesday at 5 P.M. ET for our Facebook live math help session. https://www.facebook.com/KathleenJasperEdD.

Check out my other products.

I have built several comprehensive, self-paced online courses for many teacher certification exams. I also have other books, webinars and more. Go to https://kathleenjasper.com and use offer code **SPED20** for 20% off any of my products.

Join my private Facebook group.

Are you trying to become a teacher and are you looking for a community? Share insights, strategies and connect with other prospective teachers.

Go to: www.facebook.com/groups/certificationprep/ to request access.

Subscribe to my YouTube channel

Check out my enormous video library with tons of interesting and insightful content for teacher certification exams and more.

Subscribe here https://www.youtube.com/kathleenjasperedd.

If you have any questions, don't hesitate to reach out. It will be my pleasure to help.
Good luck on your exam.

–Kathleen Jasper, Ed.D.

This page intentionally left blank.

Table of Contents

This page intentionally left blank.

Often people will purchase a study guide and become overwhelmed with the amount of information and tasks within the guide. Below is a suggested way to use the book.

Step 1: Use the practice test at the end of the guide as a pretest. Do this first to measure your skills. This will be a baseline score.

- Take the practice test.

- Mark the ones you get incorrect, but DO NOT look at the correct answers or explanations. That way you can reuse this test later.

- Record your score. This will be your raw score out of 120 because there are 120 questions on the practice test.

- Determine the subareas and objectives in which you are low.

Step 2: Begin your studies with your strengths and weaknesses in mind.

- Start with Content Category I.

- Read the information under each section. That information is very important.

- Work through all the information in the sections in the guide.

- Complete the 10 practice problems at the end of each content category. If you get less than 80% correct, go back through and review content category.

- Do this for all sections of the book.

Step 3: Once you've worked through the entire guide, take the practice test again.

- Work backward starting with the answer choices first. Eliminate bad words, focus on good words. Then read the question stem.

- Check your answers and read ALL the answer explanations. There is a ton of information in the answer explanations, so even if you get the answer correct, read the explanation.

- Review information as needed.

QUICK TIPS: These tips are represented with a megaphone and include tips and vocabulary you need to know or strategies for answering questions for a particular skill or content category.

 TEST TIPS: Test tips are represented with a light bulb and are specific test taking strategies that can be, and should be, used while taking the exam.

 THINK ABOUT IT: These tips are not necessarily tested concepts, but they provide background information to help make sense of concepts and give necessary information to help answer questions on the exam.

 CAUTION: Caution tips explain what to avoid when selecting your answer choices on the exam. Test writers are very good at creating distracting answer choices that seem like good options. We teach you what to watch for when it comes to *distractors* so you avoid these pitfalls.

Don't forget to look over the reference pages

I have included a Good Words List before practice test one. This is a list of words, terms, and phrases that are typically in correct answer choices on this exam. There is also a Bad Words list, which contains words and phrases to avoid. Use the list to ***think like a test maker, not a test taker*** and to be strategic on the exam.

I have also included a reference sheet that includes eminent authors, major works, and dates. This will help you with questions that are specific to certain authors included in the literary canon.

The Praxis® Special Education: Core Knowledge and Applications 5354 is designed to assess standards-based knowledge of skills and competencies of special education teachers. The assessment is comprised of 5 content categories. The following table provides an overview of the assessment.

Test at a Glance	
Test Name	Special Education: Core Knowledge and Applications
Test Code	5354
Time	2 hours
Number of Questions	120 selected-response questions
Format	Selected response
Test Delivery	Computer delivered

Content Category	Approx. Number of Questions	Approx. Percentage of Exam
I. Development and Characteristics of Learners	20	16%
II. Planning and the Learning Environment	27	23%
III. Instruction	27	23%
IV. Assessment	22	18%
V. Foundations of Professional Responsibilities	24	20%

Terms You Need to Know for the Exam

- Individualized Education Program may be referred to as an IEP.

- Attention-deficit/hyperactivity disorder may be referred to as ADHD.

- The Individuals with Disabilities Education Act may be referred to as IDEA.

- A multidisciplinary team or Child Study Team may be referred to as an IEP team.

- A teacher assistant, teacher aide, or paraeducator may be referred to as a paraprofessional.

- The No Child Left Behind Act may be referred to as NCLB.

- A biological parent, legal guardian, surrogate, natural, adoptive, or foster parent may be referred to as a parent.

- The term "students with intellectual disabilities" is used to refer to students previously referred to as "students with mental retardation." As used in this test, the two terms refer to the same group.

- Students with emotional and behavioral disturbances may be referred to as EBD.

- Autism spectrum disorder may be referred to as ASD.

- Resource room is a special education room where individualized services and instruction are provided to students.

- RTSI/MTSS are methods that include interventions and supports for student BEFORE they are labeled as needing special education services.

- Inclusion means including special education students in mainstream or general education classes.

- LRE means the least restrictive environment and supports inclusion and educating special education students with their nondisabled peers.

A. Human development and behavior

B. Theoretical approaches

C. Defining characteristics of major disability categories

D. Impact of disabilities on individuals, families, and society

E. Language, cultural, and gender differences in the identification process

F. Co-occurring conditions

G. Family systems

H. Environmental and societal influences

A. Human development and behavior

Children go through developmental stages as they grow. It is important that special education teachers know these stages so they can spot typical and atypical cognitive, physical, and emotional development in children.

Piaget – Stages of Cognitive Development

Perhaps the most widely used framework when analyzing child development is Piaget's stages of cognitive development. Piaget asserted that cognitive development was a reorganization of mental processes resulting from biological maturation and environmental experience.

Piaget's 4 Stages of Cognitive Development		
Sensorimotor	0–2 years	Children at this stage figure out the world through sensory and motor experiences. Object permanence and separation anxiety are hallmarks of this stage.
Pre-operational	2–6 years	Children at this stage identify and use symbols for objects but do not have the ability to apply logical reasoning. They know how to pretend and are egocentric.
Concrete operational	7–12 years	Logical reasoning about concrete objects kicks in during this stage. Conservation, reversibility, serial ordering, and understanding cause and effect relationships are hallmarks of this stage, but thinking is still limited to the concrete.
Formal operational	12 years–adult	Abstract thinking such as logic, deductive reasoning, comparison, and classification are demonstrated by the individual in this stage.

(Piaget, 1972)

Atypical Child Development

Atypical development means a child does not develop normally. This can result in developmental disabilities. Developmental disabilities are a group of conditions due to a physical, neurological, learning, language, or behavior impairment. These conditions impact day-to-day functioning and usually last throughout a person's lifetime (Rubin and Crocker, 1989).

B. Theoretical approaches

Behaviorist theory influences how teachers create engaging learning experiences and manage classroom behaviors. This is especially important in special education. In this section, we will explore terms and concepts of motivational theories that you may see on the exam. On the exam, you will relate a learning or teaching scenario to a concept or theory or, conversely, apply a theory to a classroom management, learning, or instructional situation.

Motivation theory

The best teachers motivate students by designing and delivering engaging and relevant instruction. Increasing special education students' motivation, regardless of disability, is a common theme on the exam. These types of test questions will be presented as scenarios, and you will be expected to choose the most effective approach. The best teachers motivate all students—high-achieving, low achieving, culturally diverse, and economically diverse students. Effective teachers use many motivational tools in their instruction and learning environment when needed.

Self-determination

Self-determination is the ability to make decisions for oneself and to control one's own future. A student with strong self-determination is motivated by opportunities to collaborate on instructional design, set goals for themselves, and navigate obstacles to succeed. The application of self-determination theory is best understood through intrinsic motivation.

Self-advocacy

Self-advocacy is speaking up for oneself and expressing needs and wants. This is very important in special education because as students get older, they will have to express their needs for accommodations so they can thrive. Teaching students to do this at an early age will serve them later in life when they are on their own.

Intrinsic motivation

Intrinsic motivation is behavior driven by internal rewards rather than external rewards. According to self-determination theory, intrinsic motivation is driven by three things: autonomy, relatedness, and competence.

Test Tip

Look for answer choices on the exam that promote student's self-advocacy – speaking up for oneself and expressing needs and wants. It is very important that students with disabilities learn to advocate for themselves, so they receive the instruction and accommodations they deserve.

- **Autonomy.** This has to do with students' independence and self-governance. Allowing students to decide how and what they learn helps to increase autonomy and increase motivation. Students should be permitted to self-select books and work on things that interest them.

- **Relatedness.** Students must see the value in what they are learning as it pertains to their everyday lives. The best teachers make learning relatable and applicable to the real world.

- **Competence.** Students must feel they are equipped to meet your expectations. It is important to challenge students while also providing students with activities based on readiness levels and ability.

Extrinsic motivation

Extrinsic motivation refers to behavior that is driven by external rewards. Providing students with a party if they reach their reading goal or allowing students extra playtime because they cleaned up the classroom are examples of extrinsic motivation. Grades can also be considered extrinsic rewards. Extrinsic motivation is often unsustainable because once the reward is removed, the student is no longer motivated to achieve.

Contingency-Based Classroom Management

Contingency-based classroom management makes students responsible for managing their own behavior. This type of classroom management provides rewards for appropriate or positive behaviors. Group contingency is where the teacher reinforces the entire class or a smaller group of students for completing tasks, engaging in appropriate classroom behaviors, or exhibiting other targeted behaviors. Group contingencies are most often used as a basic classroom management strategy. Studies have shown group contingencies decrease inappropriate behavior and increase prosocial behavior in special education classrooms and, in some instances, improve school-wide indicators of success (Hansen & Lignugaris/Kraft, 2005).

Other Approaches to Student Learning and Motivation

Desensitization is a technique where a person is exposed to small doses of an anxiety-inducing stimulus alongside of a relaxation technique. This is used in reinforcement theory in which there is a weakening of a response, usually emotional, used to change a behavior. For example, for a student with social anxiety, the teacher may bring the student to a corner of the playground and help the student with relaxation techniques, so the student becomes less anxious during playtime.

Extinction is a technique where the teacher removes the reinforcement for a problem behavior. In order to decrease or eliminate occurrences of these types of negative (or problem) behaviors. For example, a young student uses tantrums during lunch because she doesn't want to eat her food. If the teacher puts the student in timeout (a reinforcement), the tantrums will continue because going to timeout eliminates lunchtime. Instead, the teacher ignores the tantrums and continues to insist the student eat her food during lunch. Eventually the tantrums will decrease because the student is not receiving a desired outcome from the tantrums.

Manipulating the Antecedent Stimulus – A type of intervention that changes the student's behavior by manipulating conditions that *precede* such behavior. For example, arranging the layout of the classroom so students are less likely to cause disruptions. This involves:

- Presenting the cues for the desired behavior in the child's environment.

- Arranging the environment or setting up a biological condition so that engaging in the desirable behavior is more valuable to the child.

- Decreasing the physical effort needed for the child to engage in the desired behavior.

Manipulating the Consequent Stimulus – A type of intervention that changes student's behavior by manipulating conditions that *follow* such behavior. For example, when a student misbehaves, the student receives timeout or another consequence. This is often referred to as punishment.

Planned Ignoring – When a teacher identifies undesirable behaviors used for attention and then ignores those behaviors. This reduces undesirable behaviors.

Premack Principle – Also known as the first-then principle. A teacher using the Premack Principle says, "First clean up your centers, then we can go on the playground."

Satiation – When an extrinsic reward loses its effectiveness. For example, giving students candy every time they clean up after playtime as a reward starts to lose its effectiveness over time because students get sick of the candy. This is why extrinsic rewards are often unsustainable over time.

C. Defining characteristics of major disability categories

There are many types of disabilities students face, and it is the special education teacher's job to identify these disabilities and accommodate each student based on the student's individual needs. No two people are exactly the same, even if they have the same disability. Therefore, understanding each disability and how they impact students individually is essential in providing students with a free, appropriate public education (FAPE).

Developmental Delay vs Developmental Disability

A developmental delay is something a student can grow out of. For example, with enough speech therapy and practice, a student can work through speech delays. However, a developmental disability is something a student will not grow out of. For example, if a student has cerebral palsy, he or she will not be able to eradicate that disability with therapy. The student can live a fulfilling life and achieve academically. However, the student will have cerebral palsy for life.

According to the CDC, recent estimates in the United States show that roughly one in six, or 17%, of children aged 3 through 17 years have one or more developmental disabilities. These include:

1. **ADHD** – People with ADHD may have trouble paying attention, controlling impulsive behaviors (may act without thinking about what the result will be), or be overly active. Although ADHD cannot be cured, it can be successfully managed, and some symptoms may improve as the child ages.

2. **Autism spectrum disorder** – Autism spectrum disorder (ASD) is a developmental disability that can cause significant social, communication and behavioral challenges. The learning, thinking, and problem-solving abilities of people with ASD can range from gifted to severely challenged. It is a spectrum disorder, meaning there is a range of challenges for people with ASD. Some people with ASD require full-time care in their daily lives; others need therapy and do not need full-time assistance.

3. **Cerebral palsy** - Cerebral palsy (CP) is a nondegenerative condition—meaning it does not get worse over time—that affects a person's motor skills and balance. CP is the most common motor disability in childhood. It is estimated that 1 in 345 children are born with CP. The cause of CP is brain injury that occurs before, during, or immediately after birth.

4. **Hearing loss** – Hearing loss can affect a child's ability to develop communication, language, and social skills. The earlier children with hearing loss start getting services, the more likely they are to reach their full potential.

5. **Intellectual disability** – An intellectual disability limits a person's ability to learn at an expected level and function in daily life. Levels of intellectual disability vary greatly in children. Children with an intellectual disability might have a hard time letting others know their wants and needs. They also may not be able to take proper care of themselves. Students with intellectual disabilities often need assistance when learning to speak, walk, dress, or eat.

6. **Learning disability** – Learning disabilities are disorders that affect the ability to understand or use spoken or written language, complete mathematical calculations, coordinate movements, or direct attention. Types of learning disabilities include:

   - Dyscalculia affects a person's ability to understand numbers and learn math facts.

   - Dysgraphia affects a person's handwriting ability and fine motor skills.

   - Dyslexia affects reading and related language-based processing skills.

   - Non-verbal affects the ability to interpret nonverbal cues like facial expressions or body language and may cause poor coordination.

7. **Vision impairment** – Vision impairment is any kind of vision loss.

8. **Behavior disability** - An emotional disability characterized by the following:

   - An inability to build or maintain satisfactory interpersonal relationships with peers and/or teachers.

   - An inability to learn, which cannot be adequately explained by intellectual, sensory or health factors.

   - Consistent or chronic inappropriate type of behaviors or feelings under normal conditions.

   - Displayed pervasive mood of unhappiness or depression.

   - Displayed tendency to develop physical symptoms, pains or unreasonable fears associated with personal or school problems.

Think about it!

Fine motor skills require coordination in the small muscles of the hands, wrists, and fingers.

Gross motor skills require coordination in the large muscles of the legs, arms and torso.

D. Impact of disabilities on individuals, families, and society

According to the CDC, 61 million—or 1 in 4 adults—live with a disability. That's 26% of the population. (Center for Disease Control, 2018). Caring for those with disabilities places demands on individuals, families and society. Some families need special equipment or vehicles for disabled children. Others need special services throughout their lives. Schools are where disabled students receive the necessary services for a free, appropriate public education (FAPE). However, the day-to-day care for someone who is disabled can often lead to physical and emotional exhaustion for both the caregiver and the person with the disability.

E. Language, cultural, and gender differences in the identification process

Often, students who are English language learners (ELLs) are disproportionately represented in special education programs and are labeled learning disabled when they do not have a learning disability, and instead are struggling with the language. Misidentified students are likely to encounter limited access to a rigorous curriculum and diminished expectations. More importantly, mislabeling students creates a false impression of the child's intelligence and academic potential. This is important for several reasons.

- Once students are receiving special education services, they tend to remain in special education classes (Harry & Klingner, 2006).

- Students are likely to encounter a limited, less rigorous curriculum (Harry & Klingner, 2006).

- Lower expectations can lead to diminished academic and post-secondary opportunities (National Research Council, 2002; Harry & Klingner, 2006).

- Students in special education programs can have less access to academically able peers (Donovan & Cross, 2002).

- Disabled students are often stigmatized socially (National Research Council, 2002).

F. Co-occurring conditions

When two or more disorders occur at the same time, they are called co-occurring disorders or comorbidity. The most common comorbid relationship is between learning disabilities and attention deficit disorder hyperactivity (ADHD).

When other disorders are present, it can make the diagnosis of ADHD much more difficult to pinpoint and the symptoms harder to treat. Some comorbid disorders that commonly occur alongside ADHD are:

- Oppositional Defiant Disorder
- Conduct Disorder
- Depression
- Anxiety
- Bipolar Disorder
- Learning Disorder
- Autism
- Sensory Integration Disorder
- Early Speech/Communication problems

Studies suggest that anywhere from 24% to 52% of students with learning disabilities have some form of such a disorder (DiPasquale, n.d.).

Quick Tip

Sometimes students who do not know how to express anger will rely on passive aggression. Passive-aggressive behavior is a deliberate but covert way of expressing feelings of anger (Long, Long & Whitson, 2009). Passive aggression is motivated by a young person's fear of expressing anger directly.

G. Family systems

More than 1.5 million children in the United States are estimated to have an intellectual disability (Federal Interagency Forum on Child and Family Statistics, 2009). Positive feelings toward children with intellectual and developmental disabilities may be associated with a broader optimistic outlook. An optimistic perspective will help promote well-being and safeguard parents from the harmful effects of stress and depression usually associated with caring for someone with a disability.

Teachers should play a role in this optimism. Things teachers can do are:

- Focus on the students' strengths.

- Call home with good news.

- Celebrate gains with the student and parents.

- Help parents with strategies to positively interact with children with special needs.

H. Environmental and societal influences

There are many environmental and social influences on student development and achievement. Perhaps the most widely known theorist who addressed this is Abraham Maslow in the hierarchy of needs.

Abraham Maslow

Maslow is widely known for the Hierarchy of Needs (as shown below). Maslow asserted that people are motivated by 5 basic factors: physiological, safety, love, esteem, and self-actualization. According to Maslow, when a lower need is met, the next need on the hierarchy becomes the focus of attention. If students are lacking a lower need, they cannot be motivated by one of the other needs. For example, if a student does not have basic needs like food or shelter, the student will not be motivated by esteem. Food and water are fundamental to all the other needs.

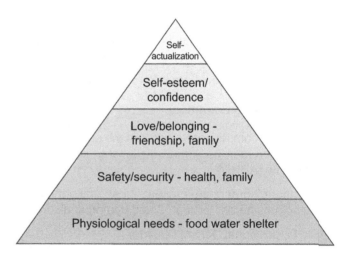

- **Maslow in the classroom**

    - Meeting students' needs before moving on to high-level assignments/activities.

    - Considering students' situations at home before assigning work.

Quick Tip

Core qualities of life include emotional, physical and material well-being, social inclusion, and human rights.

1. A teacher is having a hard time motivating her special education students to settle down during cooperative learning. The students are often disruptive and unfocused. She decides to reward each group with extra time on the playground is they settle down and complete their cooperative activity. What tactic is the teacher using?

   A. Extrinsic rewards and group contingency

   B. Intrinsic rewards and individual accountability

   C. Intrinsic rewards and group contingency

   D. Extrinsic rewards for individual accountability

2. John is a visually impaired student in an inclusive math class. The class is working on attributes of three-dimensional shapes. Which of the following accommodations would be most effective for John in this situation?

   A. Give John line drawings of three-dimensional shapes.

   B. Allow John extra time on tests and quizzes for the unit.

   C. Give John manipulatives of three-dimensional shapes.

   D. Allow John to work with a partner during the unit.

3. A teacher tells students that when they finish the assignment on the board, they can take a break and play outside, the teacher is using:

   A. Satiation

   B. Premack Principle

   C. Planned ignoring

   D. Manipulated antecedent stimulus

4. A teacher is trying to motivate a special needs student to exhibit appropriate behaviors during reading time. The student continues to call out and seek attention. What should the teacher do?

   A. Threaten to call home and let the student's parents know about the situation.

   B. Ignore the behavior, continue with the reading, and praise students who exhibit appropriate actions.

   C. Offer the student a reward if the student behaves.

   D. Send the student to time out until the student exhibits the appropriate behavior.

5. Which of the following is considered a developmental disability?

   A. A student has delayed speech until 6th grade.

   B. A student has trouble reading on grade level without assistance.

   C. A student is exhibiting atypical growth.

   D. A student has ADHD and needs accommodations.

6. Which of the following should be considered when analyzing the quality of life of a 17-year-old student with special needs?

    A. Fine motor skills

    B. Gross motor skills

    C. Social interaction

    D. Diet and nutrition

7. A 10th grade student with special needs is working with her IEP team to develop annual goals. She is interested in setting new goals and letting the team know what she wants out of her education. The student is exhibiting (Check all that apply):

    A. Self-assessment

    B. Self-regulation

    C. Self-advocacy

    D. Self-determination

8. Which of the following describes a co-occurring behavior or a comorbid behavior?

    A. A student with ADHD is also displaying signs of bipolar disorder.

    B. Two students with the same disability start to act similar in their behaviors.

    C. A student drops one bad behavior for another.

    D. When a student is rewarded for bad behavior and continues to display that behavior.

9. This affects a person's ability to understand numbers and learn math facts.

    A. Dyscalculia

    B. Dysgraphia

    C. Dyslexia

    D. Non-verbal

10. Which of the following would not be an effective strategy to motivate students?

    A. Using group contingency

    B. Lower standards so the assignments are easier.

    C. Using intrinsic rewards

    D. Using manipulatives

Number	Answer	Explanation
1.	A	Extra time on the playground is an extrinsic reward. She is also using group contingency because the group gets the reward if the group works together to complete their cooperative learning assignment.
2.	C	If John is visually impaired, allowing him to use concrete models of the three-dimensional shapes to touch is most effective here. Line drawings are least effective because John will have a hard time seeing them. Working with a partner and extra time on quizzes do little to help him in this situation.
3.	B	Think of the Premack Principle as a if – then statement. If you finish your work, then you can go on the playground.
4.	B	Because the student is seeking attention, the teacher should remove that reward from the situation. Answers A, C and D all reward the negative behavior because the teacher in those situations is giving the student attention. Ignoring the behavior and giving attention to students who are behaving is the most effective choice for this situation.
5.	D	Answers A, B and C can be considered developmental delays. Only answer D is considered a disability.
6.	C	Core qualities of life include emotional, physical, and material well-being, social inclusion, and human rights. Improving students' social skills is a positive theme on this exam.
7.	C & D	Students with strong self-determination are motivated by opportunities to set goals for themselves and navigate obstacles to succeed. Self-advocacy is sticking up for oneself and letting people know what one needs. Answers A and B are not good choices here because self-assessment and self-regulation has to do with the student evaluating oneself and regulating one's own behavior. That is not what is outlined in the scenario.
8.	A	Co-occurring or comorbid behaviors are when two or more disorders occur at the same time.
9.	A	• Dyscalculia affects a person's ability to understand numbers and learn math facts. • Dysgraphia affects a person's handwriting ability and fine motor skills. • Dyslexia affects reading and related language-based processing skills. • Non-verbal affects the ability to interpret nonverbal cues like facial expressions or body language and may have poor coordination.
10.	B	Lowering the standards in the classroom is never the correct practice. Therefore, choice B is the answer.

This page intentionally left blank.

II – Planning and the Learning Environment

A. Effective lesson planning

B. Measurable objectives

C. Access to the curriculum

D. Organizing the learning environment

E. Managing student behavior

F. Effective classroom management

G. Design and maintenance of a safe and supportive classroom environment

A. Effective lesson planning

Lesson plans help to guide and focus instruction. Special education teachers must use lesson plans to organize time, resources, and instruction to maximize learning for students. When lesson planning for special education, using backward design is most effective. In backwards design, the teacher starts with the standard or goal the teacher wants students to achieve and then plans the lessons according to that standard or goal.

BACKWARD DESIGN

When planning lessons, backward design is very effective. The key to backward design is to start with the state standards and work backward.

Alignment is critical. Start with the standards, plan the assessments, monitor the students' progress at key intervals, and adjust short-term objectives accordingly.

Steps to Backward Design

1. Identify the state-adopted standards for the concepts you are teaching. Be sure you are following the scope and sequence outlined by the state standards. The goal is student mastery of the standard(s).

2. Choose what assessments you will use to determine if the students mastered the standard(s).

3. Plan the lesson and activities.

4. Monitor progress as students move through the unit, lesson, or activity.

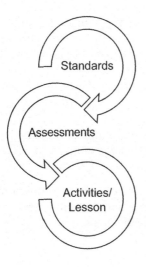

Standards
Assessments
Activities/ Lesson

- Start with the state adopted standards. That is the end goal–to have the students master the standard(s).

- Determine how you will know the students mastered the standard and what assessments you will use to measure success.

- Decide what lessons and activities you will have students engage in to work toward standards mastery.

State Standards

The most important element of an effective lesson plan is standards alignment. Teachers must consider the academic standards as the guiding characteristics of lessons and activities. The state has laid out the standards it expects students to achieve. Students are often tested on these standards on state exams in reading, writing, and math at the end of each year. Therefore, using the standards to drive instruction is most effective in lesson planning and design.

Vertical alignment occurs when lessons and activities in the classroom support one grade level to the next or one skill to the next. The standards are vertically aligned—every skill in each standard supports one grade level to the next. For example, the skills outlined in the standards for 7th grade math are designed to help students prepare for what they will need in 8th grade math, 9th grade math, and so on. While the standards are designed to be vertically aligned, it is the responsibility of the educator to ensure students are receiving lessons that are vertically aligned. Educators can vertically align their lessons by:

- Collaborating with other teachers in professional learning communities (PLCs).
- Paying close attention to the standards that come before and after the year being taught.
- Attending professional development that focuses on standards alignment.

Horizontal alignment occurs when lessons are aligned to other academic disciplines and content areas. For example, 9th grade social studies teachers plan with the 9th grade English teachers to design a common lesson focusing on the Civil Rights Movement. This lesson will fulfill social studies standards in U.S. history and English language arts standards in reading and writing. This relationship between the two content areas to focus on common content, goals, and standards is horizontal alignment. Effective educators can be sure lessons are horizontally aligned by:

- Collaborating with other teachers in professional learning communities (PLCs).
- Researching other content areas that relate to the content being taught.
- Looking for connections where curriculum can support other content areas.

Measurable Objectives

Learning objectives are the behaviors or skills students are expected to acquire in a lesson. These objectives should be measurable, meaning teachers should be able to determine if the objective is met either by a formative or summative assessment. We will discuss assessment in the following sections. Measurable objectives allow teachers to determine if students understand the lesson and are meeting the standards.

Flexibility

Another important element of effective lesson plans is fluidity. Lessons do not always go according to plan. For example, it may take longer than expected for students to understand a concept or complete and activity. Therefore, lesson plans should be flexible, and teachers should modify the lessons according to students' needs.

B. Measurable objectives

Objectives detail what a student will be able to do by the end of the learning activity. Objectives should be measurable because teachers have to determine if the objectives of learning were met before moving onto the next lesson.

Effective teachers don't just write the learning objective on the board; they communicate the objective to the students and use the objective to guide instruction and learning throughout the lesson. Effective teachers regularly check in with students to communicate learning objectives.

Objectives contain three main components.

1. The skill or behavior to be performed.

2. The conditions under which the students will perform the skill or behavior.

3. The criteria used to measure the objective.

Think about it!

Teachers write objectives on the board before the lesson, so students understand what skills and behaviors are expected at the end of the lesson.

Here is an example of a well-written objective that is aligned to the state standards for middle grades life science: *At the completion of unit 3 – cell functions, students will apply their knowledge of cell structures and functions by writing an expository essay and scoring at least a 3 out of 4 based on the assigned rubric.*

Notice that the objective above contains all 3 components:

1. The skill or behavior performed – students will apply their knowledge.

2. The conditions under which the students will perform the skill or behavior – writing an expository essay.

3. The criteria used to measure the objective – scoring a 3 out of 4 based on the rubric.

PLANNING AND THE LEARNING ENVIRONMENT

Bloom's Taxonomy

Bloom's Taxonomy is a hierarchical model used to classify educational learning objectives into levels of complexity and specificity. The higher up the pyramid, the more complex the thinking skills. The skills are represented as verbs on the pyramid. When answering questions on the exam about objectives, remember Bloom's Taxonomy.

IMPORTANT: The figure shown is a modified version of Bloom's Taxonomy. We have modified it to include other skills (verbs) you may see on the exam.

The skills (verbs) at the highest points of the pyramid are apply, analyze, evaluate, and create. When you are faced with a critical thinking problem on the test, visualize this pyramid, and look for answer choices that reflect the higher portions of the pyramid.

Create

Analyze

Evaluate

Apply

Compare & Contrast

Categorize

Understand & Identify

Remember & Memorize

Example Problem

Which of the following would be the most effective science activity to increase critical thinking?

A. In cooperative groups, students analyze different textures of rocks and generate questions.

B. As teams, students identify types of rocks based on certain characteristics like hardness and texture.

C. As a class, students go outside and collect and categorize different rocks.

D. Students read about rocks in the textbook and answer comprehension questions.

Correct Answer: A

In this scenario, choice A has the term *analyze*. Analyze is at the top of the pyramid; therefore, it is related to critical thinking. Also, generating questions is an activity associated with critical thinking. Choices B and C use words like identify and categorize, which are not associated with critical thinking. Answer choice D is a typical non-answer on exam. While individual reading and answering questions is an activity a lot of teachers use in the classroom, it is usually not the correct answer on the test. Be sure to focus on the verb and not the activity to determine the answer. All of these activities can be effective, but the verb in the sentence indicates the cognitive complexity level.

Measurable Goals

Goals are different from objectives in that goals are usually bigger milestones and they often govern longer periods of time. For example, an objective is something a student can achieve in one class period while a goal is something the student may achieve over a semester or school year. Objectives are certainly incremental goals. It is worth mentioning here that goals, like objectives, should be measurable. The best way to ensure the goals you and your students set are measurable is to use the SMART goal method.

When drafting goals, it is helpful for students and teachers to use the SMART method. SMART stands for **S**pecific, **M**easurable, **A**chievable, **R**elevant, and **T**imely.

Specific. The goal must contain a statement that details specifically what the student will accomplish.

Measurable. There must be a way to measure progress towards the goal—using assessment data.

Achievable. The goal must be within the scope of abilities of the student.

Relevant. The goal must be relevant to what the student is doing in school/life.

Timely. The goal must be completed within a targeted time frame.

Examples of SMART goals:

- By the end of the quarter, Patricia will increase written language skills by using proper spelling and punctuation in 4 out of 5 trials with 80% accuracy as measured by formative assessments.

- By the end of the semester, Jocelyn will increase her fluency from 93 words per min to 125 words per minute as measured by informal fluency reads.

Ways to Track and Measure Students' Goals

Data folders. Students use data folders to track their progress by recording their achievements. Teachers and students reference data folders throughout the year to progress monitor, set new goals, and conduct student-led conferences. This is an example of teachers and students using data together to make decisions.

Portfolios. A student portfolio is a compilation of academic work and other forms of educational evidence assembled for the purpose of:

- Evaluating coursework quality, learning progress, and academic achievement.

- Determining whether students have met learning standards or other academic requirements for courses, grade-level promotion, and graduation.

- Helping students reflect on their academic goals and progress as learners.

- Creating a lasting archive of academic work products, accomplishments, and other documentation.

Compiling, reviewing, and evaluating student work over time can provide an authentic picture of what students have learned and are able to do.

Progress monitoring. Teachers and students progress monitor by continuously looking at data, both qualitative and quantitative, to measure academic improvement. Teachers progress monitor by using ongoing formative assessments to measure students' skills throughout the learning process.

C. Access to the curriculum

Providing students with disabilities access to the general curriculum is mandated under the Individuals with Disabilities in Education ACT (IDEA). Instructional supports, inclusive classroom practices, parent involvement, appropriate accommodations and modifications, updated IEPs, are all examples of helping these students access general education curriculum.

For the exam and for your special education classroom, make sure you know common strategies for helping special education students access the general education curriculum:

- Help students with their social skills because social skills are necessary for general education and cooperative learning.

- Differentiate instruction because that addresses a student's learning profile, which includes learning style, environmental factors that affect the student's learning, and the student's grouping preferences.

- Read students' IEPs and plan instruction according to their needed accommodations and their academic and behavioral goals.

- Keep standards high while also providing accommodations and modifications to help students access and meet those standards.

- Use common modifications to activities and assignments to help students achieve their goals. These include giving students extra time, using small groups for assignments, allowing students to use audio components or large print, and using sensory tools.

D. Organizing the learning environment

Setting up well-organized, well-defined learning spaces helps special education students in the classroom. According to the Global Educator Institute (2015), there are 7 critical areas for arranging the special education classroom. This is just one way to set up your classroom. Teachers must be able to modify this environment depending on students' needs. Formatively assessing how this set up is serving students and rearranging accordingly is very helpful too.

- **Home Base**: This is the individual student's space. It should be clearly marked with the student's name. This is where the student completes independent work. A student can go to home base to prepare for or review the day's events, escape stress or anxiety and regain control, work on independent activities, or prepare to transition to the next activity. Setting up each student with a home base is critical for child-oriented teaching models.

- **Group Area**: This is often split into two areas — one for whole-group instruction and the other for small groups. Whole group is usually teacher driven when the teacher is giving instruction to the entire class. The small-group area is where students work in cooperative learning centers or work in small, teacher-led groups.

- **Sensory Area:** This is a space dedicated to addressing your students' sensory needs. Bean bag chairs, rugs, stress balls, weighted pads or blankets are items that may be found here.

- **Student Schedule Area**: This is dedicated space, either on the wall, door, or a shelf, for a visual schedule. Use words and pictures to illustrate each activity. You may also find that using arrows is helpful for students to plan and prepare for transitions in activities. Use different colors or label them *first* and *then*. Using this area can help you be explicit in how the class should transition from one activity to another, and it also helps students be successful in meeting these expectations.

- **Reading Center:** This is a quiet, secluded spot where students can read independently or with a partner. It is very helpful to have comfortable seating in this area.

- **Writing Center:** This is where students write independently or with others. Make sure there is enough room and access to supplies.

- **Teacher Zone:** This is where teachers have their own space to check school emails, plan lessons, store records, etc. While most of the classroom real estate should be devoted to students, having your own small area is just as crucial. This can also be a good teaching tool for students to understand boundaries.

When it comes to organizing the classroom, flexibility is very important. If certain things aren't working, consider redesigning and rearranging. It may take several iterations of design to get the right fit for you and your students. Finally, don't forget to include your students in the discussion. Students are an invaluable resource when it comes to input for classroom design.

E. Managing student behavior

Student behavior should be approached the same way student learning is approached. Teachers must observe behavior, collect data on that behavior, and then devise a plan of action. Sending students to detention does not fix a behavior problem. Learning about the behavior and differentiating the approach to the behavior is most effective.

Behavior Tips:

- *Observe the behavior first.* Before a teacher can prescribe punishment or a solution to the behavior, she must first observe the behavior. These observations yield necessary data the teacher should consider before moving forward. Determine the frequency—how often the behavior occurs—and latency—the time in between behavior occurrences.

- *Come up with a plan.* Using an evidenced-based approach, begin to design a plan of action. Allow the student to be a part of behavior plans. Allowing students to set behavior goals and devise a plan on how to attain them helps students take ownership of the process.

- *Contracts work.* Using positive language, come up with an agreement you and the student can live by. Help the student outline a goal. Let the student be part of the construction of the contract. Revisit the contract to celebrate gains and to make new goals.

Positive Behavioral Interventions and Supports (PBIS)

Positive Behavioral Interventions and Supports (PBIS) is an evidence-based, three-tiered framework for improving and integrating all of the data, systems, and practices affecting student outcomes every day. It is a way to support everyone – especially students with disabilities – to create the kinds of schools where all students are successful.

PBIS includes tiered intervention systems. Positive behavior support focuses on the positive behaviors rather than punishing the negative behaviors. The following information was taken from the Center on PBIS tiered framework.

Tier 1: Universal Prevention (All)

Tier 1 supports serve as the foundation for behavior and academics. Schools provide these universal supports to all students. For most students, the core program gives them what they need to be successful and to prevent future problems.

Tier 2: Targeted Prevention (Some)

This level of support focuses on improving specific skill deficits students have. Schools often provide Tier 2 supports to groups of students with similar targeted needs. Providing support to a group of students provides more opportunities for practice and feedback while keeping the intervention maximally efficient. Students may need some assessment to identify whether they need this level of support and which skills to address. Tier 2 supports help students develop the skills they need to benefit core programs at the school.

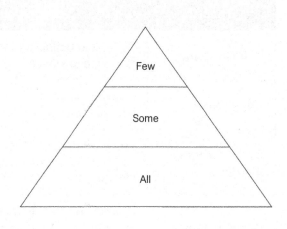

Tier 3: Intensive, Individualized Prevention (Few)

Tier 3 supports are the most intensive supports the school offers. These supports are the most resource intensive due to the individualized approach of developing and carrying out interventions. At this level, schools typically rely on formal assessments to determine a student's need and to develop an individualized support plan. Student plans often include goals related to both academics as well as behavior support.

Behavioral Data Collection. Data-driven decision making is when a teacher collects data, analyzes the data, and then makes a decision based on the data. Observing a behavior before deciding how to move forward is data-driven decision making. Observations, journal entries, surveys, interviews, etc. yield important information teachers can use to be effective when applying intervention strategies.

Adolescent Behavior

Adolescence is a time for developing independence. Adolescents typically exercise their independence by questioning and sometimes breaking the rules. During this time students are trying to develop an identity, gain acceptance from peers, and develop competence. The most common function of behavior displayed by adolescents is avoidance coping or avoidance behaviors. Avoidance behaviors are ways of behaving that are motivated by the desire to avoid certain thoughts or feelings. The behaviors will include avoiding places or situations such as school or social events.

Most districts have moved from a top-down, punitive system of dealing with behavior, to a restorative justice, positive behavior management system. The research shows that positive behavior support yields better results than a system focused on punishments.

Caution

When looking at test questions having to do with student behavior, any answer choice that sounds negative or punitive is probably **NOT** the correct answer choice. Avoid negative or punitive answer choices.

F. Effective classroom management

Effective classroom management has its roots in several theories. While you will most likely not be asked about specific theorists on the exam, it does help to understand the foundational theorists of behavior and apply these early theories to the practice of classroom management.

Theory	Definition	Example
Behaviorism	Observing behaviors that are a response to stimuli.	System of external rewards for good behavior.
Cognitivism	Focuses on intellectual growth and how students learn.	Asking students to track their reading progress in a data folder.
Social learning theory	Proposes that new behaviors can be acquired by observing and imitating others.	A teacher models appropriate speaking and listening behaviors and students emulate those behaviors.
Constructivism	Learning is a result of your experiences and what you bring to the learning.	The teacher has a limited role and students are in charge of their learning.

Edward Thorndike

Thorndike was one of the earliest behaviorists. He is best known for his connectionism theory that outlines three main learning laws emphasizing rewards, repetition, and signs of readiness.

John Watson

John Watson said that human behavior can also be explained by classical conditioning. Watson observed that humans can be conditioned to associate tastes, noises, positive feelings, and negative feelings with cues from their environment.

B.F. Skinner

Skinner's operant conditioning theory is based upon the idea that learning is a function of change in overt behavior. Changes in behavior are the result of an individual's response to events (stimuli) that occur in the environment. A reinforcer is anything that strengthens the desired response. It could be verbal praise, a good grade, or a feeling of increased accomplishment or satisfaction. External rewards are often associated with Skinner' learning theory.

Abraham Maslow

Maslow is widely known for the hierarchy of needs. Maslow asserted that people are motivated by 5 basic factors: physiological, safety, love, esteem, and self-actualization. We mentioned Maslow in content category one of this book. There you can find a diagram of his hierarchy of needs.

Most effective Classroom Management

The most effective classroom management usually is focused on increasing positive behaviors and decreasing negative behaviors. While external rewards do work in the short-term, intrinsic rewards are much more sustainable and yield better results. For example, if you are constantly rewarding good behavior with candy, students will eventually tire of the candy. However, if students feel fulfilled when they exhibit positive behavior, they are more likely to continue that behavior.

Also, using a democratic approach to classroom management is very effective. This means that the teacher involves the students in setting expectations for the class. Students are more likely to meet expectations they help put in place rather than ones imposed on them top down. Remember, classroom management should be positive.

G. Design and maintenance of a safe and supportive classroom environment

It is important that the classroom environment adapt to the needs of students. For example, if some students have ADHD and have a hard time concentrating, then the teacher can remove distractions from the environment or plan to seat those students where there are fewer distractions. The following are some important aspects of a safe and supportive classroom.

Routines

All students, not just those with disabilities, benefit from routines in the classroom. Having an idea of what is expected every day and knowing what to expect every day is comforting to people. Chaos and surprises do little to help anyone. Therefore, establishing classroom routines help students and teachers to feel safe in the classroom

Procedures

Procedures go along with routines and help students to understand what is expected at different times. For example, when transitioning from math block to reading block, there should be set procedures in place. When using equipment or walking to the lunchroom, there should be procedures in place. In addition, procedures must be practiced over and over again, so students are able to execute procedures for each activity. Procedures should be in place before any teaching or learning occurs.

Teaching Approaches

Often in a special education classroom, teachers will have the opportunity to work with another professional or teacher in the same room. For example, a teacher and a paraprofessional may work together in a math class. Two teachers may work together in an elementary classroom. Having more than one instructor can be beneficial to a supportive classroom environment. The following are some examples of coteaching approaches.

- **Co-teaching** – the practice of pairing teachers together in a classroom to share the responsibilities of planning, instructing, and assessing students. Co-teaching is often implemented with general and special education teachers paired together as part of an initiative to create a more inclusive classroom.

- **Station Teaching** – the approach of having an instructor at each center or station. This promotes small group and individualized instruction for specific skills.

- **Alternative Teaching** – a co-teaching model where one teacher works with a small group of students as the other teacher instructs the large group. This approach allows teachers to maximize the amount of time spent on differentiation and scaffolding techniques.

- **One Teach, One Assist** – the method where one teacher has the responsibility to deliver main instruction while the other teacher walks around the room and assists. The assist teacher may help students get supplies or help clarify if students have questions.

- **One Teach, One Observe** – the method often used for data collection. The main teacher instructs the lesson, and the other teacher observes students and collects formative data.

- **Parallel Teaching** – A method involving two teachers who divide the class in half and teach the same thing to each respective half of the class.

- **Team Teaching** – the method involving two teachers in front of the class sharing the responsibility of whole-group instruction.

Another way in which teachers can help students thrive in the classroom is to plan for activities that promote learning for all different students with different needs and preferences. The following is a table with several types of approaches teachers can use.

Activity	Definition	Example
Jigsaw	A cooperative learning activity in which each student or groups of students read and analyze a small piece of information that is part of a much larger piece. They then share what they learned with the class.	Teachers arrange students in groups. Each group reads and analyzes a piece of a text. Group members then join with members of other groups, and each student shares and discusses his or her section of the text. As the group shares, the entire text is covered. It is referred to as Jigsaw because students complete the puzzle when they share their individual pieces.
Chunking	A reading activity that involves breaking down a difficult text into manageable pieces.	In a science class, students break down a lengthy and complex chapter on genetics by focusing on pieces of the text. The teacher has planned for students to read and analyze the text one paragraph at a time.
Think-Pair-Share	A cooperative learning activity in which students work together to solve a problem or answer a question.	Think – The teacher asks a specific question about the text. Students "think" about what they know or have learned about the topic. Pair – Students pair up to read and discuss. Share - Students share what they've learned in their pairs. Teachers can then expand the "share" into a whole-class discussion.
Reading Response Journals	A writing activity where students use journals to react to what they read by expressing how they feel and asking questions about the text.	After reading a chapter of a book in class, the teacher asks students to use their reading response journals to respond to the story emotionally, make associations between ideas in the text and their own ideas, and record questions they may have about the story.
Evidence-Based Discussion	The teacher sets the expectation that students use evidence in the text to support claims they make during the discussion.	The class is discussing World War II. Students are asking and answering questions. When making claims, students identify support for those claims in the text.
Literature Circles	A small-group, cooperative learning activity where students engage and discuss a piece of literature/text.	In their cooperative groups, students read and analyze text together. Each student contributes to the learning. There is an administrator who decides when to read and when to stop and discuss. There is a note taker who writes down important information. There are 2 readers who take turns reading the text based on the administrator's suggestions.

1. A teacher is observing a student who is continuously disruptive during reading time. The teacher tallies 7 times in 15 minutes that the student disrupts during reading time. What is the teacher trying to determine with this approach?

   A. Frequency

   B. Latency

   C. Duration

   D. Intensity

2. Carla is a student with an emotional behavior disorder (EBD). She frequently becomes overwhelmed when transitions occur in class. She will often act out or not participate when there is a transition from one activity to the next. What can the teacher do to help Carla with classroom transitions?

   A. Call home and let Carla's parents know that she is not following directions in class.

   B. Ask the principal to provide a paraprofessional to help Carla with classroom transitions.

   C. Build classroom routines and practice procedures regularly with Carla.

   D. Pair Carla with a student who understands the classroom routines and procedures.

3. Ms. Setters is building her lesson plans for the week for her 4th grade special education class. Where would the following statement belong in the lesson plan?

   Students will identify types of rocks and how they are formed?

   A. Materials needed

   B. Objectives

   C. Accommodations

   D. Duration

4. Ms. Johnson often includes students in decision-making sessions for the class. For example, they class decided on new classroom expectations for the semester. They also voted on several books to be included in the classroom library. Which of the following best describes this approach?

   A. Reciprocal teaching where the teacher is the facilitator and students are in charge.

   B. Democratic classroom management for increased buy-in and increased self-esteem.

   C. Direct instruction where the teacher is doing most of the work and the students are compliant.

   D. Small-group instruction where students receive differentiated instruction and individualized learning.

5. A teacher has several students who are hearing impaired. What can the teacher do to ensure that all students are able to understand the instructions for each assignment?

   A. Have students copy down all the instructions for each assignment and activity.

   B. Pair hearing impaired students with visually impaired students.

   C. Send all instructions home in paper form.

   D. Be sure to face the class while giving instructions and provide written instruction when necessary.

6. Which of the following is most effective when helping students achieve their behavior goals in their IEPs?

    A. Reward good behavior with extra time on the playground.

    B. Pair students who struggle with those who follow directions.

    C. Set clear expectations for classroom behavior.

    D. Threaten to call home if students misbehave or break classroom procedures,

7. Ms. Jones is a special education teacher with many of her students having behavioral disabilities. She uses a system of rewards and consequences. The expectations are clearly stated on the wall, and she and the students go over them before each day starts. Which of the following is most effective in this type of classroom management strategy?

    A. Give all rewards and consequences by the end of the day.

    B. Allowing students to pick their own consequences when they do not meet expectations.

    C. Allow students to choose which expectations they want to meet each day.

    D. Deliver rewards and consequences immediately after the behavior happens.

8. Jean is a 10th grade student with an intellectual disability. According to her last assessment, Jean is functioning at a 5th grade level. Jean's teacher allows her to decide what books she reads and encourages her to examine her own experiences and how they affect her learning. The teacher is using which theoretical approach?

    A. Behaviorism

    B. Cognitivism

    C. Social Learning

    D. Constructivism

9. In a 5th grade special education classroom there are two teachers. One teacher is taking a large group of students and going over the procedures for an upcoming lab. The other teacher has a small group of students and is reinforcing concepts they will need to understand in order to work through the lab properly. What type of teaching method is this?

    A. Alternative teaching

    B. One-to-one teaching

    C. Parallel teaching

    D. Station teaching

10. A teacher is modeling speaking and listening skills before students engage in a class discussion about an upcoming school event. The teacher wants to show students how to effectively engage with one another while using manners and respect. The teacher is relying on what theoretical framework?

    A. Behaviorism

    B. Cognitivism

    C. Social Learning

    D. Constructivism

Number	Answer	Explanation
1.	A	The number of times a behavior occurs is the frequency. Latency is the amount of time between behaviors. Duration is how long the behavior goes on for. Finally, intensity is the strength or concentration of the behavior. Because the teacher is tallying the behavior, the teacher is determining the frequency or how many times the behavior occurs.
2.	C	Routines and procedures are always a great place to start when addressing behavior. Students, especially those with emotional disorders, find comfort in routines and procedures. To help students be successful, it is important to practice routines and procedures.
3.	B	The statement is an objective because it identifies what students are expected to do by the time the lesson is over.
4.	B	When students are given the opportunity to vote on decisions, that is a democratic classroom, which helps to increase self-esteem because students take control of their own learning. They are empowered.
5.	D	Answer D is the most reasonable and effective practice in this situation. Many visually impaired students need to see a person talking to make sense of what is being said. In addition, written instructions will also help. Answer A is busy work and will take up valuable instructional time. Answers B and C are not effective in this situation.
6.	C	Setting clear expectations for behavior is always the best approach even over rewards and incentives.
7.	D	Rewards and consequences should be given immediately after the behavior. Otherwise, the effect of the reward or consequence is lost.
8.	D	Constructivism is the theory that learning is a result of your experiences and what you bring to the learning. Teachers play a limited role in this theoretical approach.
9.	A	Alternative teaching is a co-teaching model where one teacher works with a small group of students, as the other teacher instructs the large group. This approach allows teachers to maximize the amount of time spent on differentiation and scaffolding techniques.
10.	C	Social learning theory proposes that new behaviors can be acquired by observing and imitating others. The teacher is modeling the behavior she is hoping students will imitate when they engage with others.

This page intentionally left blank.

III – Instruction

A. Appropriate strategies/techniques

B. Instructional strategies for ensuring individual academic success

C. Instructional strategies that facilitate maintenance and generalization

D. Research-based interventions for individual students

E. Implementation of supplementary and/or functional curriculum

F. Assistive technology

G. Transition goals

H. Prevention and intervention strategies

A. Appropriate strategies/techniques

When teaching students with disabilities, teachers must use instructional approaches, activities and interventions that are developmentally appropriate and help to accommodate all learners. Teachers must consider students' physical abilities along with their intellectual and behavioral capabilities. For example, a student may require a wheelchair and not have control or use of her hands; however, she may also have high-level cognitive skills and require challenging content and material. The teacher must meet the specific needs of every student.

There are several instructional approaches teachers can use in the special education and general education classroom.

- **Metacognitive** – teaching students to think about their thinking and plan, monitor, evaluate and make changes to their own learning behaviors.

- **Diagnostic Prescriptive -** identifying the most effective instructional strategies for children who differ on any number of variables believed to be related to academic learning. This requires teachers to analyze formative and summative data and apply particular methods and interventions to meet the needs of a particular student.

- **Direct instruction** – a teacher-directed method that involves the teacher standing in front of the room giving directions or modeling a lesson. This is usually done as a whole-group activity.

- **Cooperative learning** – students working together in small groups to complete tasks, analyze text, work in labs, etc. The students are in charge of their learning in this method and the teacher is a facilitator.

- **Multiple-modality** – involves providing diverse presentations, and experiences of the content so that students use different senses and different skills during a single lesson. Often multiple modalities address different learning preferences.

In a student-centered environment, teachers pay attention to learning preferences, readiness levels, and developmentally appropriate practices. Below are considerations when designing a student-centered or learner-centered classroom environment.

- **Visual learners.** These students thrive when the learning is accompanied by images and graphics to organize information.

- **Auditory learners.** These students grasp concepts best through listening and speaking situations (think lectures and podcasts).

- **Kinesthetic leaners.** These students prefer hands-on learning experiences and moving their bodies.

- **Read and write learners**. These students prefer reading and writing activities to make sense of abstract concepts.

Howard Gardner's Multiple intelligences

Another way you may see multiple modalities represented on the exam is through Garner's multiple intelligences. The following diagram outlines Gardner's multiple intelligences.

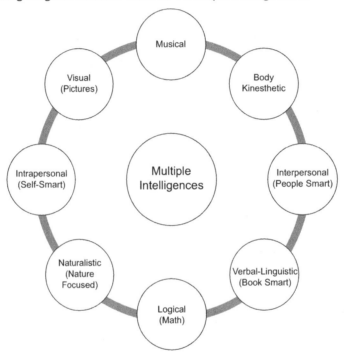

B. Instructional strategies for ensuring individual academic success

Flexible grouping can be used to accommodate students with different interests and abilities. Teachers should continuously switch student groups based on different needs or preferences students have at any given time. Flexible grouping is a term that covers a wide range of grouping students for delivering instruction such as whole class, small group, and a partner.

- Heterogeneous grouping is used when objectives are appropriate for the range of learners in the classroom. Homogeneous grouping is used to customize specific instruction for assessed student needs.

  - *Homogeneous Groups.* Everyone is the same. For example, a teacher groups all level 3 readers together. Homogenous groups should not be used regularly. **Done mostly with EBD students**.

  - *Heterogeneous Groups.* Diversity within the group. For example, grouping students by interest rather than reading scores will provide more diversity among the group members.

- Group size and composition are adjusted to accommodate and reflect student progress and instructional objectives.
- Tutoring with a peer, adult, or both are used to supplement explicit teacher-delivered instruction. The practice should align with classroom objectives and instruction.
- Cross-class or cross-grade grouping is used when appropriate to maximize opportunities to tailor instruction to students' performance levels. This is appropriate when teaching students within a similar age span and achievement range.
- Centers and independent activities should be aligned with instructional goals and objectives focused on achieving grade-level standards.

Direct instruction

Direct instruction is straight-forward and sequential instruction delivered to students from the teacher. It is useful for introducing and explaining important knowledge and concepts. The following are examples of direct instruction used in K-6 classrooms.

Direct Instructional Strategies	Purpose	Example
Explicit teaching	Usually done through direct instruction, the teacher is clearly showing students exactly what is expected.	Before an activity, the teacher writes expectations on the board and explains students' responsibilities.
Drill and practice	Repetition of a specific set of facts. The intention is memorization.	Call and response practice of spelling words, phonemes, word patterns, math facts, or steps in a process.
Lecture	Speaking to students on a topic, typically using power point presentations, dry erase or chalk board, or other visuals as props.	Introducing a social studies topic such as events leading to the Civil Rights Movement.
Demonstrations	Showing students a process, concept, or idea.	Demonstrating a science experiment. Modeling learning behaviors such as revising a piece of writing using a document camera.
Guides for reading, listening, viewing	Teacher-written guides used by students who are reading, listening, or viewing new material. The guides typically include previewing vocabulary, summarizing main ideas, and questioning to check for comprehension.	A guide for viewing a video being shown on photosynthesis. A "cause and effect in narrative writing" guide used by students as they listen to an episode of a mystery podcast.

Indirect instruction

This comes from constructivism or the idea that students derive and construct their own meaning from experiences. As an instructional practice, it means teachers are responsible for creating an environment for meaningful learning experiences to happen. Indirect instruction is considered student-driven instructional model.

Indirect Instructional Strategies	Purpose	Examples
Problem solving	Inclusive of many higher order thinking strategies including creative, critical, and analytical thinking. Allows students to apply learning by identifying problems and various solutions.	Math word problems. Finding the problem in a story and suggesting several possible solutions before reading to the end. Peer-resolution groups or playground representatives; students who are designated for helping their peers to resolve disagreements and disputes.
Inquiry	Students explore, ask and seek answers to why and how things happen.	Using KWL charts and *Think, See, Wonder* routines. Asking and pursuing answers to phenomena of the natural world. Exploring numerical concepts or find the most efficient method for solving problems.
Case studies	Case studies are a type of problem-based learning. Researching or finding insight into a topic by looking deeply at one case or situation. Students can watch a short video or read a text to learn and find context about a case.	Reviewing global issues like schooling for girls or child labor. Tackling community questions like, *How can we start a student government for our school?* Or *What do we need to create a class garden?*
Concept mapping	A graphic display of information on a topic to contextualize and connect concepts. They are especially useful for visual learners.	Reviewing lecture notes. Contextualizing research from various sources. Summarizing a process or relationships between ideas such as food chains or life cycles.
Reading for meaning	Strategies for making sense of complex text. Prompts students to preview, search for significant information while reading and reflect after reading.	Analyze: • Math word problems • Charts, graphs • Article or short story
Cloze procedures	Assessing comprehension or understanding by supplying most of a paragraph or sentence and asking students to complete the rest.	Using verbs, nouns, or other parts of speech. Recalling the details of a short story or reading.

Independent instruction

These are learning opportunities directed by students. Students are seeking out specific knowledge and developing self-regulation skills. The teacher's role is having appropriate time and materials prepared and classroom structures in place for on-task work. Like indirect-instruction, independent instruction is considered student-driven instructional models.

Independent Instructional Strategies	Purpose	Examples
Learning contracts	A voluntary agreement, usually in writing, between a student(s) and teacher about what tasks will be completed and by what time.	"I will" statements for: completing work, staying on task, contributing to group projects, and being prepared with comments for class discussions.
Research projects	To explore and present information about a chosen topic of interest	Student choses a topic within a class theme of study.
Computer mediated instruction	Any instruction and learning that involves computers or technology.	Complete a Webquest. Write a story in a shared document. Watch informational videos. Use a QR code to locate research materials.
Learning centers	Short and contained learning tasks that students can manage by themselves and in small groups. Learning centers may be thematic or differentiated to meet student learning preferences and needs.	During a reading workshop, a class is set up for students to rotate in small groups to 1) read independently, 2) listen to reading, 3) solve phonic pattern puzzles, and 4) read with the teacher.
Distance learning	Virtual or online learning can be synchronous (live with a teacher directing the lesson) or asynchronous (recorded lessons and student directed). Students may be listening and learning with the teacher in real time or have a list of tasks to complete on their own time accompanied by explanations or video instructions.	A student cannot come to school because they have an autoimmune disorder, so the student uses computer-driven lessons at home.

Experiential and virtual instruction

Experiential learning is learning by doing. This means learning tasks where students are actively engaged socially, physically, and mentally in the learning taking place. They often include going on field trips, acting out scenarios, and creating projects. This is also a student-centered instructional model.

Experiential and Virtual Instructional Strategies	Purpose	When you might use it
Field trips	Experiencing and connecting to content in a new way. Providing a shared experience for the class to reflect and process classroom learning.	A trip to the zoo before beginning (or after) a unit on animals and their habitats. Virtual field trips are a good substitute for real field trips when resources and time are unavailable.
Experiments	Developing, implementing, and understanding the process for proving claims and hypothesis. Students use problem-solving, inductive reasoning, and higher order thinking in the process of setting up and conducting experiments.	Building ramps that make cars go faster and farther. Consider what happens when combining different substances.
Simulations	A situation where an environment is designed for students to experience a scenario or setting. The idea is for them to interact and glean meaning from the experience.	Oregon Trail is a stimulus game entailing the hardships and realities of exploring the landscape and natural resources of the northwest in the early 20th century. Setting up an event, time, or place for students to have an experience. Pretending to be planets orbiting the sun.
Role play	Pretending to be characters in a story, time, place, or event to better appreciate specific feelings, perspective, and experience.	Acting out a scene from a novel. Role playing an event from U.S. history. Children having a disagreement on the playground with positive and negative outcomes.
Games	Games help students understand concepts, practice them, and engage with classmates. They can be cooperative and competitive.	Whole group math games practicing skip counting, place value, and number fluency. Scavenger hunts. Small group concept review games such as organizing words by their root word and finding places on a map.
Observations	Observing the learning behaviors of another person or class. Recall social learning theory and the significance of modeling. These observations are self-motivated and initiated.	Watching a builder construct a house. Observing animals on a farm or navigating in the wild.

Interactive instruction

Interactive instruction is learning by interacting with other people. This includes student-to-student, student-to-teacher, and teacher-to-student interaction. Instruction is student-centered with social interaction as the key component.

Interactive Instructional Strategies	Purpose	Examples
Brainstorming	Collect many ideas at once, engage students in a new topic, or begin an inquiry.	KWL charts. Asking students to think of types of transportation or names of reptiles.
Cooperative learning groups	Students work on a project or task together.	Book clubs. Experimenting with building materials to make a sturdy bridge.
Interviews	To hear an expert opinion or new perspective.	Gathering information for an essay on community or an autobiography Conducting surveys to collect and analyze data.
Discussions	Discussions are a way of co-constructing knowledge with students, checking for understanding, gauging student interest, and diving deeper into a topic. Useful across the curriculum.	Discussing why a math problem is wrong and how to fix it. Discussing cause-effect in a novel. Discussing engaging topics such as how to help stray animals.
Peer practice	To discuss a text, students work in small groups, alternating role of teacher and students. They cycle through the tasks of predicting, questioning, clarifying, and summarizing in any order.	Guided reading groups. Reading a text to prepare for a science activity. Learning new content on a social studies topic.
Debates	These are discussions with at least two clear sides to an issue. They are used like discussions but also entail preparation to defend and address counter arguments to strong argument.	They can be used to improve comprehension of a text, understand multiple perspectives to an issue, or prepare for argumentative essay writing.

C. Instructional strategies that facilitate maintenance and generalization

Strategies that support maintenance and generalization are important in any classroom, but they are very important in the special education classroom.

Maintenance strategies are those that reinforce practice of a skill that students have previously learned. Maintenance helps them retain the skill. Students with learning disabilities require lots of maintenance activities. For example, practicing site words is a maintenance skill. Students regularly practice site words, so they have automaticity in their reading.

Generalization strategies are those that help students perform a skill in a variety of settings and situations. This is sometimes referred to as transfer because students can transfer the skill from one activity to another. For example, when students learn to read letters on a chart, they will need support in applying that skill to books and signs that are not directly related to the chart. In upper grades, students may learn a science concept and then need strategies to support that concept in a lab application.

D. Research-based interventions for individual students

Students have different needs when it comes to interventions. Teachers can use interventions informally to set students up for success in the classroom. Interventions are based on a child's needs. Interventions:

- Supplement the general education program.
- Use evidence-based strategies and techniques.
- Help students improve a skill or learn to apply existing skills to new situations.

Accommodations are changes to teaching or testing that removes barriers and provides equal access to learning. Unlike a modification, it doesn't change *what* a child is learning. It changes *how* a child is learning.

For example, students with ADHD benefit from accommodations like seating arrangements where they are sat where there are few distractions. This is an accommodation a teacher can employ to mitigate distractions before they happen.

It is helpful to understand the difference between accommodations and interventions. The following table outlines the distinction.

	Interventions	Accommodations
How they are used:	Interventions are used to teach the skills kids need to improve a specific area of weakness. Once those skills are gained, interventions are removed.	Students with an Individualized Education Program (IEP) or a 504 plan have formal accommodations included in their plans. They may or may not continue to get those supports throughout their school years.
What they should include:	Targeted assessments as strategies for specific skills students are struggling with. A plan to monitor progress should also be included.	Practices that remove barriers to learning. Accommodations can be assistive technologies, testing conditions, and timing modifications.
Examples	A system of scaffolding to support students who struggle. Frequent formative assessments (these will be covered in the next section) to measure students' skills. Differentiated instruction (small-group and 1-1 academic support) when needed.	Seating students away from distractions. Alternative testing environment. Permitted use of notes, number lines and other aids during classroom assessments. Assistive technology like screen readers or voice to text devices.

Quick Tip

All of the interventions and accommodations students receive in school should be used with an inclusive model in mind. Inclusion aligns with providing students with the least restrictive environment (LRE). LRE is part of the Individuals with Disabilities Education Act (IDEA) that says children who receive special education should learn in general education as much as possible. Keep LRE in mind when answering questions on the exam.

E. Implementation of supplementary and/or functional curriculum

When the needs of a special education student are not met in the general education classes, supplementary or functional curriculum may be necessary. Implementing supplementary or functional aids should be used to keep students in LRE and educated as much as possible with their peers who are not in special education. Remember, the goal is inclusion, so supplementary and functional curriculum is there to keep students in the general classroom as much as possible.

Supplementary curriculum and aids are services and other supports that are provided in regular education classes, other education-related settings, and in extracurricular and nonacademic settings, to enable children with disabilities to be educated with nondisabled children to the maximum extent appropriate.

Functional curriculum is a curriculum model for students with moderate and severe disabilities. Content is selected based on identified skills needed for functioning in current and future integrated community, residential, and vocational environments. The instruction for students in the moderate and severe/profound classes is based on the Curriculum Guide for Students with Intellectual Disabilities.

Functional curriculum usually centers around 4 main domains:

1. Functional Academics – Skills learned in school that can be applied in the real world

2. Personal development/ Interpersonal Skills – How to function in social situations

3. Career Development – How to prepare for employment

4. Independent Living – The skills needed to live safely and independently

Think about it!

The domains for functional curriculum are centered around teaching special education students to live independently in the real world. Just like inclusion is the goal for school, inclusion is the goal in life. Therefore, within the domains of functional curriculum are areas that focus on personal care, domestic skills, money management, safety skills, self-advocacy, and more.

F. Assistive technology

There are many types of assistive technology available to students with disabilities. From screen readers to talk-to-text software, students can bypass many barriers caused by disabilities. It is important to keep the following in mind when helping students with assistive technology.

1. Assistive technology ranges from low- to high-tech.

2. Assistive technology can be used in two ways: to support learning and to bypass a challenging task such as handwriting.

3. In order to be effective, assistive technology needs to be embedded within quality instruction.

There are many types of assistive technologies for students with disabilities. The following are a few you may see on the exam.

- **Text-to-speech or screen readers** can read aloud digital or printed text. This technology is helpful for students who are visually impaired.

- **Speech-to-text or voice recognition** can be helpful for students who do not have use of their hands.

- **Talking calculators** are helpful for students who are visually impaired.

- **Visual computer cues** are helpful for students who are hearing impaired.

- **Recording devices** are helpful for student with intellectual disabilities because they can record the lesson or lecture and replay it later to reinforce and skills they might have missed.

- **Frequency modulated (FM)** devices amplify and improve listening conditions in the classroom setting beyond that which hearing aids provide. FM equipment is usually available to students who are Deaf/HH.

Test Tip

On the exam, you will most likely encounter questions about assistive technology. It is important that you evaluate the particular disability mentioned in the question and match that to the most effective assistive technology.

G. Transition goals

The individualized transition plan (ITP) is a section of the IEP that outlines transition goals and services for students with disabilities. The ITP is the template for mapping out short-term to long-term adult outcomes from which annual goals and objectives are defined. The ITP outlines goals for students to work towards that will help them move from high school to postsecondary school and career. Because students have varying disabilities, the goals for the ITP vary based on each student. For example, some students ITP will include a plan for college while other students' plans may focus on independent living skills like cooking and hygiene.

The ITP must:

- Address the student's preferences, interests, strengths, and needs

- Outline parent participation

- Focus on specific goals

- Describe activities demonstrating use of various strategies, community and adult living experiences

- Include annual goals

- Define responsibilities of parents and students

Quick Tip

IDEA requires all students have an ITP by the age of 16. However, the transition process starts at age 14. On the exam, you will most likely have more than a few questions about the ITP process. Just like everything else, the ITP is focused on goals that will help students live a full independent life.

H. Prevention and intervention strategies

Because an inclusive classroom where students are assigned the least restrictive environment is the goal of special education, often, special education teachers must use prevention and intervention strategies to assist students with mild to severe disabilities.

Some students have health issues that cause them distress during the school day. For example, some students may have seizures throughout the school day. It is very important that teachers read students' IEPs, fully understand what is required to assist students in these circumstances, seek training when appropriate, and plan to intervene when necessary.

Prevention and intervention strategies include those that prevent undesirable behaviors or actions and promote positive behaviors and actions. These strategies include:

- **Positive behavioral interventions and support (PBIS)** is a set of research-based strategies used to increase quality of life and decrease problem behavior by teaching new skills and making changes in a person's environment. It focuses on the good behaviors and works to eliminate or reduce the bad behaviors.

- **Social skills instruction** focuses on actions and routines that help students function in an inclusive classroom, school, and environment. This instruction can also focus on conflict resolution skills which help mitigate disruptions and inappropriate behaviors.

- **Academic enrichment** helps to support students with disabilities so they can achieve their goals and contribute to the academic classroom.

Quick Tip

An occupational therapist is someone who works with students to participate in everyday activities. Not only do they promote self-esteem and value, but they also work with developing cognitive, motor, and physical skills.

INSTRUCTION

This page intentionally left blank.

1. A teacher is looking over her students' recent spelling tests and sees that 5 students are struggling with the concept of long vowel sounds when spelling their words. She decides to spend some time in a small group with these students and go over these words. Which instructional approach is the teacher taking in this siltation?

   A. Metacognitive

   B. Diagnostic prescriptive

   C. Direct instruction

   D. Whole group

Use the following scenario to answer questions 2-4.

Julie is a 12-year-old student who uses a motorized wheelchair and has limited control of her hands. She tested above grade level for reading, writing, and mathematics. Her writing was assessed orally because she has difficulty with fine-motor control. Her occupational therapy goal is to improve fine-motor control, so that she can grasp a pencil to write and use utensils for eating.

2. Which of the following accommodations would be best for Julie during a social studies cooperative learning activity?

   A. Exempt Julie from writing because of her issues with fine motor control.

   B. Allow Julie to watch a video that outlines the concepts in the activity.

   C. Pair Julie with a buddy to assist her in taking notes during the activity.

   D. Allow Julie to work on her own since she enjoys reading independently.

3. Which of the following would be the best assistive technology for Julie during an assignment that requires typing on the computer?

   A. A screen reader

   B. An expanded keyboard with large keys

   C. Noise canceling headphones

   D. Paraprofessional to read to Julie

4. Which of the following accommodations would be most appropriate for Julie during a reading assessment that requires bubbling in answers on a scantron?

   A. Having a paraprofessional bubble in Julie's dictated answers.

   B. Testing Julie in a separate room.

   C. Having a paraprofessional read the test aloud for Julie.

   D. Allowing Julie extra time on the exam.

5. Which of the following should be the teacher's goal when administering interventions or accommodations for students with special needs?

   A. Continuing interventions throughout the entire school year.

   B. Maintaining detailed records of student success.

   C. Holding students accountable for their learning.

   D. Maintaining an inclusive and least restrictive environment.

6. James, a student in Ms. Jackson's class, has frequent seizures. Ms. Jackson has read James' IEP and knows that he will probably have one or more seizures throughout the school year. What are the most appropriate steps for Ms. Jackson to take?

   A. Teach students what to do when James has a seizure.

   B. Assign James a buddy to walk James to the nurse after a seizure.

   C. Have a plan to document when seizures occur and to inform appropriate personnel.

   D. Work with the student on strategies to prevent seizures from happening.

7. Ms. Jones is a high school special education teacher working with her students on functional curriculum. Which of the following activities would benefit her students in this area? Choose all that apply.

   A. Learning to do math problems in different ways and apply those math skills to areas in science.

   B. Helping students advocate for themselves when they need assistance or special services.

   C. Reviewing skills for time management that applies to home life and work.

   D. Going over test scores and determining where students need to focus their studies.

8. Students with disabilities often receive support in social skills because:

   A. Teaching social skills is crucial for success in an inclusive classroom.

   B. Focusing on academics is not beneficial to students with disabilities.

   C. Working on social skills will help students make friends in and outside of school.

   D. Social skills are necessary in a self-contained classroom.

9. Ramona is a high school junior with specific learning disability (SLD) in reading. Which of the following should she and her teachers focus on when helping her meet her goals in her individual transition plan (ITP)?

   A. Finding an apartment in which she can safely live on her own.

   B. Researching postsecondary schools and advocating for adaptive services in her courses.

   C. Working on independent living skills like doing laundry and cooking meals.

   D. Budgeting her monthly finances.

10. Mr. Ruiz, a special education teacher, has a few students who get frustrated when working in groups. They often become confrontational and have a difficult time expressing themselves. Which of the following would be most appropriate for Mr. Ruiz to employ with students?

    A. Design a whole-group lesson on the importance of teamwork and how to apply that in the classroom.

    B. Call the students' parents and inform them about the students' behavior and ask for their help in disciplining the students.

    C. Set up a system of consequences for students who misbehave and a system of rewards for those who act appropriately.

    D. Work with these students in a small group to develop a plan for expressing themselves, conflict resolution and positive behavior support.

Number	Answer	Explanation
1.	B	In this example, the teacher diagnosis the problem and then prescribes a solution or strategy to solve the problem. Therefore, answer B is correct.
2.	C	Because Julie has trouble with fine motor skills, pairing her with a buddy to assist in the writing portion of the cooperative learning activity is most effective. Answers A and D are incorrect because exempting Julie from the activity excludes her from classroom expectations, which is never the correct answer. Answer B does nothing to help Julie in this situation.
3.	B	Because Julie has special needs regarding her fine motor skills, she will need a special keyboard with large keys. Answer A would be an accommodation for someone who has vision impairment. Answer C and D would not help Julie with her fine motor skills needs.
4.	A	Because Julie's main struggle is fine motor skills, she may have trouble bubbling in answers on a scantron. If the teacher is assessing Julie's reading skills, then having a paraprofessional bubble in the answers Julie dictates is the most appropriate accommodation for Julie.
5.	D	Inclusion and LRE are the goals in special education. While students may need accommodations, those accommodations should be used in an inclusive environment. Continuing interventions all year is incorrect because if interventions are no longer needed, they should be removed. Answer choices B and C are good practices. However, inclusion and LRE beat out all other answer choices on the exam. If you see LRE or inclusion in an answer choice, slow down and consider that it is probably the correct answer.
6.	C	The only appropriate action listed in the answer choices is answer C. The teacher should have a plan to document the seizure and inform proper personnel.
7.	B & C	Functional curriculum is about skills students need to live and independent life outside of school. In answer B, the activity is outlining self-advocacy, a skill necessary for special education students to thrive in the real world. In answer C, the activity is time management, which is also a skill necessary for work and homelife. Answers A and D are only academic skills.
8.	A	Remember, inclusion is a good word on this exam. Therefore, when you see it in an answer choice, it is most likely the correct answer. In this case, an inclusive classroom is the goal, so answer A is correct.
9.	B	Ramona is a junior with a reading disability. This is a minor disability, and therefore, she should be focusing on college. She will also need to focus on advocating for herself to receive services to which she is entitled. All of the other answer choices are for someone with severe disabilities.
10.	D	Answer D is a proactive approach to the situation. In addition, students are more likely to follow expectations when they are included in developing expectations. Finally, answer D has all the good words in it: expressing oneself, conflict resolution, and positive behavior support.

INSTRUCTION

This page intentionally left blank.

IV – Assessment

A. Evidence-based assessments

B. The use of various assessments

C. Data-based decisions using assessment results

A. Evidence-based assessments

Effective special education teachers use a variety of assessments to measure student progress. In the special education classroom, there are specialized assessments that measure students' abilities and determine if students need special services.

Behavior Assessment System for Children (BASC) or Vineland Adaptive Behavior Scale

This assessment measures behavior and mental health, including how students see themselves as well as how parents and school staff see the students. These evaluations do not offer a diagnosis but instead look at life skills, social skills, social concerns, and attention. This assessment may help identify mental-health concerns and/or behavioral issues.

Functionality: School Function Assessment (SFA)

The SFA measures a student's functionality in all areas of the school environment. The occupational therapist (OT) administers this assessment. This test evaluates three areas: participation, task support, and activity performance. It is usually used for students in kindergarten through grade 6. It addresses not only classroom access but also playground, lunch, physical education, and other school areas.

The Present Levels of Academic Achievement and Functional Performance (PLAAFP)

The purpose of the PLAAFP is to identify the type and amount of special education a student receives. The PLAAFP must include a statement of the child's present levels of academic achievement and functional performance, including how the disability impacts the individual's involvement and progress in the general education curriculum or participation in age-appropriate activities.

Woodcock-Johnson Psycho-Educational Battery, Third Edition

This assessment provides a comprehensive set of individually administered tests to measure cognitive abilities, scholastic aptitudes, and achievement. This is an assessment used to determine if a student has a learning disability.

Functional Behavioral Assessment (FBA)

This type of assessment is a process for identifying problem behaviors and developing interventions to improve or eliminate those behaviors. For example, A school psychologist may conduct a functional behavior assessment and find that the student uses profanity or pushes other students when lining up for lunch. These behaviors can be identified, and the teacher and school psychologist can choose appropriate interventions to help replace undesirable behaviors with appropriate behaviors.

Think about it!

Intellectual disabilities and learning disabilities are different. Intellectual disabilities include deficits in life skills, such as social interaction, taking care of oneself, and functioning in the real world. Learning disabilities have to do with academics. Be sure you distinguish between the two on the exam.

B. The use of various assessments

Teachers can use a variety of assessment tools to monitor students' progress towards learning goals. An **assessment tool** is the actual instrument (test, rubric, survey, etc.) that is used to collect data that allows a teacher to monitor student progress. Assessments may be given paper and pencil style, through the use of technology, informally by a show of hands, verbally, or in various other formats. A variety of assessments is important when progress monitoring in order to collect the most meaningful data about student progress of learning goals, as defined by state standards.

Progress Monitoring

In the special education classroom, it is imperative that the teacher continuously monitors students' progress. This will help the teacher make decisions that benefit each student based on specific needs. As previously mentioned, this is done in both a formal manner and informal manner. For example, a teacher might use a quick formative assessment, such as an exit ticket, to determine if students are understanding a particular skill or concept. A teacher may also use test scores that measure several concepts to measure progress over time, such as with STAR testing or district quarterly testing. The following are a variety of assessment tools teachers can use to monitor student progress, achievement, and learning gains.

Assessment Type	Definition	Example
Diagnostic	A pre-assessment providing instructors with information about students' prior knowledge, preconceptions, and misconceptions before beginning a learning activity. Diagnostic assessments are considered formative assessments because they inform instruction.	Before starting a science unit, a teacher gives a quick assessment to determine students' prior knowledge of concepts in the text. She uses this information to make instructional decisions moving forward.
Formative	A range of formal and informal assessments or checks conducted by the teacher before, during, and after the learning process in order to modify instruction.	A teacher is walking around the room, checking on students as they work through math problems, and intervening when necessary. The teacher uses this observational data to make instructional decisions.
Summative	An assessment that focuses on the outcomes. It is frequently used to measure the effectiveness of a program, lesson, or strategy.	A teacher gives a unit exam to measure outcomes and the effectiveness of instructional strategies.
Performance-Based	An assessment that measures students' ability to apply the skills and knowledge learned from a unit or units of study: the task challenges students to use their higher-order, critical thinking skills to create a product or complete a process.	After reading text about the Civil War, students develop stories about different historical figures in the war. Students then perform these stories in front of the class and answer questions.

Assessment Type	Definition	Example
Portfolio	A purposeful collection of student work that has been selected and organized to show student learning progress over time. Portfolios can contain, samples of student work, self-evaluations/reflections, etc.	Over the course of a semester, students collect weekly writing samples and organize them by date in a designated folder. During parent conferences, students show their parents the portfolio and reflect on progress.
Criterion-Reference	An assessment that measures student performance against a fixed set of predetermined criteria or learning standards. Most commonly known criterion-reference exams are state standardized assessments.	At the end of the spring semester, students take the state test in reading and writing. The state uses the scores for accountability measures.
Norm-Reference	An assessment or evaluation that yields an estimate of the position of the tested individual in a predefined population with respect to the trait being measured. Results are usually communicated as a percentile ranking.	The NAEP is an exam given every few years for data purposes only to compare students' reading scores across the U.S.
Screening	An assessment used to place students in appropriate classrooms or grade level.	Students are typically screened throughout the year to determine at what level they are reading. Placement decisions are made based on the outcomes of the screening.
Rubric	An assessment tool used to measure a student's performance.	Students are given rubrics to show them the expectation of the assignment or project. Then they are graded against that rubric.

ASSESSMENT

Test Tip

On the exam, summative assessments will most likely be attached to cumulative, independent activities that assess students' subject matter knowledge. For example, when students are independently completing a set of math problems after a unit, that is most likely a summative assessment.

Rubrics

A rubric is an evaluation tool or set of guidelines used to promote the consistent application of learning expectations, learning objectives, or learning standards in the classroom, or to measure their attainment against a consistent set of criteria. Rubrics are typically used for large projects and writing, but they can be used for any assignment. The following is an example of a rubric.

	1 - Minimal	2 - Meets	3 - Exceeds
Grammar and Mechanics	Many spelling, grammar, and punctuation errors; sentence fragments; incorrect use of capitalization.	Some spelling and grammar errors; most sentences have punctuation and are complete; uses uppercase and lowercase letters.	Correct spelling, grammar, and punctuation; complete sentences; correct use of capitalization.
Ideas and Content	Key words are not near the beginning; no clear topic; no beginning, middle, and end; ideas are not ordered.	Main idea or topic is in first sentence; semi-defined topic; attempts beginning, middle and end sections; some order of main idea and details in sequence.	Interesting, well-stated main idea or topic sentence; uses logical plan with an effective beginning, middle, and end; good flow of ideas from topic sentence to details in sequence.
Organization	Ideas are unorganized and do not follow a coherent structure.	Organized enough to read and understand the ideas.	Very organized and easy to understand.

Quick Tip

Rubrics should be given to students before, during, and after the assignment or task. For example, before starting a research paper, the teacher should go over the rubric with students to set expectations and communicate what students must include in the paper. During the writing process, students should use the rubric to be sure they are meeting expectations. Once students complete the research paper, the teacher should use the rubric to score the papers and provide specific and meaningful feedback.

C. Data-based decisions using assessment results

It is very important that there is someone on the IEP team who can evaluate and interpret evaluation results. Parents, the student, and other members of the team may not have the knowledge to interpret results of certain measures. Therefore, it is important that the team member tasked with interpreting results can clearly and effectively communicate the results to the parents, student and teachers. Regardless of the assessment, results should always be used to make decisions affecting the student. This is the foundation of data-driven decision making.

Think about it!

Since the goal is inclusion in the general curriculum, the student with disabilities may have general education teachers who are not experts in special education. In addition, these teachers may not know how to interpret results of different assessments specific to special education. Therefore, it is imperative that there be someone on the IEP team who can communicate results to parents, teachers, and the student so the student can achieve the goals outlined in the IEP.

Understanding how to use assessment data is key to being an effective educator. Teacher s much use assessment data to drive instructional decisions. Here are.a few ways student data is presented.

Raw Score

This is the number of questions a student gets correct on the exam. Raw scores are helpful in determining specific academic strengths and weaknesses.

Percentile Rank

A percentile rank tells how well a student performed in comparison to other students who took the same test. The percentile rank value is the percent of students the test taker scored better than on the assessment. A percentile rank of 73 means the student scored better than 73% of all the students who took the assessment. The percentile rank does not reflect how well an individual student scored or what they know. It simply compares a student to a much larger group of students to see how their performances compare.

Percentage

A percentage is based out of 100 and can translate into how many problems a student answered or did not answer correctly. For example, if a student scored a 65% on a 120-question exam, the student got 78 questions correct.

Stanine

A stanine is a scaled score that is based on a nine-point scale. This simplified scale is a way to easily group students from the lowest performers to the top performers. Stanines are another way to compare groups of students, such as percentile ranks and other types of scaled scores.

On the exam, you may encounter questions about IQ tests. Therefore, we wanted to include the following information.

Quick Tip

Qualitative data is data that cannot be quantified numerically. For example, observational notes, surveys, and interviews are types of qualitative data.

Quantitative data is data that is quantified numerically. For example, test scores, percentile rankings, and levels are types of quantitative data.

IQ Tests or Wechsler Intelligence Scale for Children (WISC)

IQ tests are used to determine if a student has a severe intellectual disability. An IQ of 20-35 means that a student has a severe intellectual learning disability. Below is a breakdown of scores for this assessment

- **Extremely Low: Below 70.** Students who test in this range may need to be placed in special education courses.

- **Very Low: 70-79.** Students who test in this range may have a learning disability and should review their subtest scores to identify specific areas of cognitive weakness.

- **Low Average: 80-89.** This is slightly lower than the mean score of 100, but still able to perform as expected in the classroom.

- **Average: 90-109.** The vast majority of children tested will score in this range with a mean (averaged) score of 100; the highest possible score on the WPPSI-IV is 160.

- **High Average: 110-119.** This typically indicates a stronger cognitive ability in one or more areas.

- **Very High: 120-129.** A score like this indicates the student is gifted in many areas required for school and testing success.

- **Extremely High: 130+.** Students who score in this range are considered academically gifted and talented.

Quick Tip

Norm-reference assessments compare student performances. The WISC test mentioned above is a norm-referenced test. Typically, norm-reference assessments provide students with a percentile ranking. For example, if a student scored in the 85th percentile, the student scored at or above 85% of the people taking the exam; the student is at the top. A student who scored in the 25th percentile only scored at or above 25% of others taking the same test; the student is at the bottom.

1. This year, students will take an exam that compares student performances to one another. Students are taking what type of assessment?

   A. formative

   B. norm-referenced

   C. criterion referenced

   D. diagnostic

2. A teacher is administering a functional behavior assessment to a student who is having outbursts during class. Which of the following is the teacher trying to determine by using a functional behavior assessment?

   A. Cognitive disabilities

   B. Effects of consequences

   C. Causes of the behavior

   D. Skills deficits

3. The classification of severe intellectual disability is determined primarily on the basis of:

   A. A score of 20-30 on the WISC test.

   B. A score of below level on the BASC.

   C. A below average score on the SFA.

   D. A below average score on the PLAAFP.

4. A teacher notices that a student is struggling to read a certain part of the text. The teacher wants to understand what specific skill the student is lacking so the teacher can address it. What assessment type would be the most effective in this situation?

   A. summative

   B. criterion-refenced

   C. norm-referenced

   D. diagnostic

5. Which of the following is the most effective way to use a criterion-referenced assessment?

   A. to compare student performances

   B. to drive instructional decisions

   C. to measure student learning at the end of a lesson

   D. to decide where to place students for class ranking

6. A formative assessment is:

   A. ongoing and used as a final grade for students.

   B. static and used as a preassessment.

   C. static and used to compare student performances.

   D. ongoing and used to determine how to move forward with teaching.

7. Which of the following provides rich qualitative data regarding student behavior?

   A. diagnostic assessment

   B. student survey

   C. anecdotal record

   D. oral assessment

8. When can teachers provide the accommodation of extra time on a state standardized criterion-referenced assessment?

   A. If the student has permission from a parent

   B. If a student has permission from the principal

   C. If the student has an IEP with the accommodation outlined in the plan

   D. If the student has a doctor's note outlining test anxiety

9. Which of the following assessments would be most effective in looking over students' progress in writing over a semester?

   A. Portfolio

   B. Criterion referenced assessment

   C. Norm-referenced test

   D. Screening

10. Which of the following is the most appropriate use of a criterion-referenced test?

   A. To measure a student's mastery of specific knowledge and skills after a unit of study.

   B. To determine a student's reading level to prescribe interventions.

   C. To rank a student's performance against other students who took the same test.

   D. To use a rubric to assess a student's performance on a group project.

Number	Answer	Explanation
1.	B	A norm-referenced assessment yields an estimate of the position of the tested individual in a predefined population with respect to the trait being measured. Use norm-referenced assessments to compare student performances as a percentile ranking.
2.	C	A functional behavioral assessment (FBA) helps to identify the causes of a behavior. This allows teachers to intervene before the behavior starts or set up the learning environment to prevent the behavior.
3.	A	Intellectual disabilities are measured by the Wechsler Intelligence Scale for Children (WISC) test. This is also known as an IQ test. The other assessments do not measure intellectual disabilities.
4.	D	The teacher is trying to diagnose the issue the student is having. Therefore, a diagnostic assessment is appropriate here.
5.	B	No matter what, assessments should be used to make instructional decisions in the classroom.
6.	D	Formative assessments are often informal, ongoing checks that help a teacher decide how to move forward in a lesson. Remember formative assessments inform the instruction delivery.
7.	C	For student behavior, observations with anecdotal notes are most effective. The anecdotes provide context and description off the student's behavior. All other answer choices do not address student behavior, rather they address student learning.
8.	C	The only way a student can receive extra time on a state test is if it is outlined as an accommodation on the IEP. The student must be ESE and have the accommodation documented in the plan.
9.	A	A portfolio showcases students' work over a period of time. In this situation, a portfolio is the most appropriate assessment.
10.	A	Criterion-referenced tests measure students' abilities against a set of standards. These tests are usually administered after students have been exposed to the skills. This type of test can also be classified as a summative assessment, because in this case, It is happening at the end of learning after students acquired the skills or standards. Using process of elimination answer B is incorrect because it describes a screening test or a formative assessment, depending on the situation. Answer C is incorrect because it describes a norm-referenced assessment. Finally, answer D is incorrect because it describes a measure for a performance-based assessment.

This page intentionally left blank.

V – Foundations and Professional Responsibilities

A. Federal definitions

B. Federal requirements for the pre-referral, referral, and identification

C. Federal safeguards of the rights of stakeholders

D. Legally defensible individualized education program

E. Major legislation

F. Roles and responsibilities of the special education teacher

G. Roles and responsibilities of other professionals who deliver special education services

H. Collaborative approaches: strengths and limitations

I. Communication with stakeholders

J. Potential bias

A. Federal definitions (IDEA.gov, 2021)

The guiding legislation for students with disabilities is the Individuals with Disabilities Education Act or IDEA. IDEA is a law that makes available a free appropriate public education to eligible children with disabilities throughout the nation and ensures special education and related services to those children. IDEA has 6 guiding principles. Be sure you know and understand these principles so you can not only answer many questions on the exam, but so you can also be an effective special education teacher. These are principles to live by if you are teaching students with special needs.

Think about it!

Part B of IDEA states that children between the ages of 3 to 21 are eligible for special education services. Part C of IDEA states that children from birth through 2 years are eligible for early intervention services.

Principle 1: Free Appropriate Public Education (FAPE)

FAPE means that educational services should be provided to students with disabilities at the public's expense, meaning parents should not have to pay for these services. These services must:

- Meet standards established by the state department of education.

- Be designed to meet the unique needs of each student.

- Continue to be provided to students who are suspended or expelled.

- Are outlined in a student's IEP.

A few aspects of Principle 1 that are very important have to do with an inclusive academic environment. For example, special education programs must:

- Be designed for the student to make progress in the general education curriculum.

- Provide a chance for students to meet challenging goals.

- Be more than a minimal benefit.

- Include related services and supports and provide for participation in extracurricular and other school activities.

- Include extended year services when necessary to provide FAPE.

Principle 2: Appropriate Evaluation

IDEA requires that a student must receive an evaluation before providing special education services to determine whether the student qualifies as "child with a disability" according to the IDEA definition. If the answer is yes, then to determine the educational needs of the student.

The following are important elements of this principle.

- Parents must give permission for evaluation and for services.

- A student must be evaluated in all areas of suspected disability.

- The evaluation should include a variety of tools and strategies to gather functional, developmental, and academic information.

- An evaluation should never be based on a single measure or assessment.

- The instruments and methods used for the evaluation must be technically sound, not culturally discriminatory, and provided in the language the child uses.

- Administered by trained and knowledgeable personnel.

- A new or updated evaluation should be conducted if there is reason to suspect a need or if the parent requests one.

- An evaluation must be conducted within 60 calendar days of the parent giving permission.

According to Principle 2, re-evaluations should occur:

- When conditions warrant new information

- When the parent requests re-evaluation

- Every three years unless both the parent and educators agree it is not necessary

Principle 3: Individualized Education Program (IEP)

An IEP is a written statement for each child with a disability that is developed, reviewed, and revised **at least once a year** by a team including educators, parents, the student whenever appropriate, and others who have knowledge or expertise needed for the development of the student's special education program. The most important part to remember about this principle is the concept of individualized because each student with disabilities has unique needs.

Quick Tip

Parents and students should be a part of the IEP team and should have meaningful involvement in drafting the goals outlined in the IEP.

The IEP must include measurable goals, offer meaningful progress, and support for functional skills in the general education curriculum.

Principle 4: Least Restrictive Environment

The IDEA requires that children with disabilities, including children in public or private institutions or other care facilities, be educated with children who are not disabled. This is referred to as least restrictive environment (LRE) and is an important concept you will see on the exam.

LRE means:

- Any placement outside the general education classroom must be justified by the child's individual disability-related needs.

- Students must have meaningful access to same age peers without disabilities, when appropriate.

- Schools must consider providing any needed services in the general education classroom and other integrated settings.

- Involvement in music, art, physical education, school trips, clubs, extracurricular and other activities must be accommodated.

- Funding is never an appropriate reason for a more restrictive placement.

- States must maintain a full range of placement options to meet the needs of children who require specialized treatment programs.

Principle 5: Parent and Student Participation in Decision Making

IDEA ensures students and parents have the opportunity to be active participants in each step of the special education process. Parents and students must be meaningfully involved in:

- The development, review, and revision of the IEP

- Educational placement decisions

- Determining what data needs to be collected during evaluation

- Reviewing evaluation data

- Transition planning and services starting by age 14

Principle 6: Procedural Safeguards

Procedural safeguards ensure that the rights of children with disabilities and their parents are protected and that they have access to the information needed to effectively participate in the process. Many of these concepts show up on the exam, so be sure to note the following.

Parents are entitled to notice in writing including:

- A parental rights notice to provide information about special education, procedural safeguards, and student and parent rights

- Notice in writing of IEP meetings

- Prior written notice whenever the school proposes to change or refuses to change the educational programming or educational placement of their child

Parents are entitled to access student records.

- They may review educational records for their child.

- They may obtain copies of educational records for their child.

- They may place a statement of correction or explanation in the student's record if it contains something they disagree with.

Parents have a variety of procedural protections they can invoke when they disagree with educators:

- The resolution facilitator process

- A mediation conference

- A formal written complaint

- A due process hearing

Test Tip

Due process is a big part of FAPE, so if you see the term *due process* in an answer choice, it is most likely the answer. Due process is a formal way to resolve disputes with a school about education or discipline issues. Parents have the right to an impartial hearing officer and to present evidence and witnesses at the due process hearing.

The 13 Disabilities Outlined in IDEA

While there are many ways in which a student can qualify for special education services and an IEP, there are 13 disabilities outlined by IDEA. These 13 disabilities often have other disabilities that fall under them. For example, cerebral palsy falls under orthopedic impairment. The following is a list of the 13 disabilities outlined in IDEA.

1. **Autism** is a developmental disability significantly affecting verbal and nonverbal communication and social interaction, generally evident before age 3, that adversely affects a child's educational performance.

2. **Deaf-blindness** is concomitant hearing and visual impairments, the combination of which causes such severe communication and other developmental and educational needs that they cannot be accommodated in special education programs solely for children with deafness or children with blindness.

3. **Deafness** is a hearing impairment that is so severe that the child is impaired in processing linguistic information through hearing, with or without amplification, that adversely affects a child's educational performance.

4. **Emotional disturbance** is a condition exhibiting one or more of the following characteristics over a long period of time and to a marked degree that adversely affects a child's educational performance: An inability to learn that cannot be explained by intellectual, sensory, or health factors.

   • An inability to build or maintain satisfactory interpersonal relationships with peers and teachers. Inappropriate types of behavior or feelings under normal circumstances.

   • A general pervasive mood of unhappiness or depression.

   • A tendency to develop physical symptoms or fears associated with personal or school problems.

5. **Hearing impairment** is an impairment in hearing, whether permanent or fluctuating, that adversely affects a child's educational performance but that is not included under the definition of deafness in this section.

6. **Intellectual disability** is significantly subaverage general intellectual functioning, existing concurrently with deficits in adaptive behavior and manifested during the developmental period, that adversely affects a child's educational performance.

7. **Multiple disabilities** is concomitant impairments (such as mental retardation-blindness, mental retardation-orthopedic impairment, etc.), the combination of which causes such severe educational needs that they cannot be accommodated in special education programs solely for one of the impairments. The term does not include deaf blindness.

8. **Orthopedic impairment** is a severe bodily impairment that adversely affects a child's educational performance.

9. **Other health impairment** is having limited strength, vitality or alertness, including a heightened alertness to environmental stimuli, that results in limited alertness with respect to the educational environment

10. **Specific learning disability** is a disorder in one or more of the basic psychological processes involved in understanding or in using language, spoken or written, that may manifest itself in an imperfect ability to listen, think, speak, read, write, spell, or to do mathematical calculations, including conditions such as perceptual disabilities, brain injury, minimal brain dysfunction, dyslexia, and developmental aphasia.

11. **Speech or language impairment** is a communication disorder, such as stuttering, impaired articulation, a language impairment, or a voice impairment, that adversely affects a child's educational performance.

12. **Traumatic brain injury** is an acquired injury to the brain caused by an external physical force, resulting in total or partial functional disability or psychosocial impairment, or both, that adversely affects a child's educational performance.

13. **Visual impairment** including blindness is an impairment in vision that, even with correction, adversely affects a child's educational performance. The term includes both partial sight and blindness.

(Authority: 20 U.S.C. 1401(3)(A) and (B); 1401(26))

Test Tip

Be sure you know these 13 main disabilities outlined by IDEA. You may get one or more specific questions about this. For example, while ADHD and cerebral palsy are both conditions where a student will get an IEP, they are not listed. ADHD is covered under other health impairment, and cerebral palsy is covered under orthopedic impairment.

B. Federal requirements for the pre-referral, referral, and identification

Pre-referral

During the pre-referral stage, it is essential that teachers use response to intervention (RTI) or a multi-tiered system of supports (MTSS). This is when teachers use supports and interventions to prevent students who should not be in special education from being erroneously classified as such.

Most districts have moved to MTSS when addressing the needs of struggling students. The MTSS framework is evidence-based and has had a significant impact on addressing the needs of struggling subgroups of students (Gordillo, 2015). Students do not have to be classified special education to receive MTSS.

- MTSS addresses academic as well as the social, emotional, and behavioral development of children from early childhood to graduation (Hurst, 2014).

- MTSS provides multiple levels of support for all learners—struggling through advanced (Hurst, 2014).

MTSS Tiered Systems	
Tier 1	This is the type of modifications or differentiated instruction *all* students get in the form of instruction (academic and behavior/social-emotional) and student supports. Tier 1 is the basic and general implementation of the core curriculum that is aligned to the state standards.
Tier 2	This is the type of modifications or differentiated instruction *some* students receive in addition to Tier 1 instruction. The purpose of Tier 2 instruction and supports is to improve student performance under Tier 1 performance expectations. This is also referred to as accommodations. The standards and expectations remain the same as Tier 1. However, accommodations are used for these students to be successful.
Tier 3	This is the type of modifications or differentiated instruction *few* students receive and is the most intense service level a school can provide to a student. Typically, Tier 3 services are provided to very small groups and/or individual students. The purpose of Tier 3 services is to help students overcome significant barriers to learning academic and/or behavior skills required for school success.

Quick Tip

RTI and MTSS are very important during the pre-referral phase. Teachers must use interventions and supports and thoroughly document those interventions and supports. Only after they have exhausted all options should a student start the referral process.

C. Federal safeguards of the rights of stakeholders

Under IDEA, there are procedural safeguards for parents and students. These safeguards are in place to protect students during the evaluation, placement, and reevaluation process. These safeguards are outlined in section B of IDEA.

According to the U.S. Department of Education (2020), There are several procedural safeguards available to parents under Part B, including:

- Independent educational evaluations

- Prior written notice

- Parental consent

- Access to education records

- The opportunity to present and resolve complaints through the due process complaint and State complaint procedures

- The availability of mediation

Test Tip

On the exam, be sure to equate safeguards with parent and student rights. The correct answer to questions about safeguards will normally have to do with parents having the right to see records, request a due process hearing, and consult outside evaluations.

D. Legally defensible individualized education program

According to IDEA, for an IEP to be defensible, goals outlined in the IEP must be clear, specific, and measurable. Defensible IEPs contain goals, assessments, services, participation, and a transition plan. More specifically, an IEP must have the following elements to be considered legally defensible.

- A statement of the child's present levels of academic achievement and functional performance, including how the child's disability affects his or her involvement and progress in the general education curriculum

- A statement of measurable annual goals, including academic and functional goals

- A description of how the child's progress toward meeting the annual goals will be measured, and when periodic progress reports will be provided

- A statement of the special education and related services and supplementary aids and services to be provided to the child, or on behalf of the child

- A statement of the program modifications or supports for school personnel that will be provided to enable the child to advance appropriately toward attaining the annual goals

- An explanation of the extent to which the child will not participate in the general education classroom or in extracurricular and nonacademic activities

- A statement of any individual accommodations that are necessary to measure the academic achievement and functional performance of the child on State and districtwide assessments

- If the IEP team determines that the child must take an alternate assessment instead of a particular regular State or districtwide assessment of student achievement, the IEP must include a statement of why the child cannot participate in the regular assessment and why the particular alternate assessment selected is appropriate for the child

- The projected date for the beginning of the services and modifications, and the anticipated frequency, location, and duration of those services and modifications

E. Major legislation

Family Educational Rights and Privacy Act (FERPA). FERPA is a Federal law that protects the privacy of student education records. The law applies to all schools that receive funds under an applicable program of the U.S. Department of Education.

FERPA gives parents certain rights with respect to their children's education records. These rights transfer to the student when he or she reaches the age of 18 or attends a school beyond the high school level (U.S. Department of Education, 2019).

Every Student Succeeds Act (ESSA).

Advances equity by upholding critical protections for America's disadvantaged and high-need students. Requires all students in America be taught to high academic standards that will prepare them to succeed in college and careers. Ensures that vital information is provided to educators, families, students, and communities through annual statewide assessments that measure students' progress toward those high standards (U.S. Department of Education, 2019).

No Child Left Behind 2002 (NCLB). NCLB was signed into law in 2002 and increased the federal role in holding schools accountable for student outcomes.

I. Title I: Improving academic achievement of the disadvantaged

II. Title II: Preparing, training, and recruiting high quality teachers and principals

III. Title III: language instruction for limited English proficient and immigrant students

IV. Title IV: 21st Century Schools

V. Title V: Promoting informed parental choice and innovative programs

VI. Title VI: Flexibility and accountability

Race to the Top (RTTT). Forty-six states and the District of Columbia submitted comprehensive reform plans to compete in the Race to the Top competition. While 19 states have received funding so far, 34 states modified state education laws or policies to facilitate needed change, and 48 states worked together to create a voluntary set of rigorous college- and career-ready standards (The White House, 2018).

The Consent Decree. Grounded in the 14th Amendment and the result of League of United Latin American Citizens (LULAC) vs. State Board of Education, the Consent Decree protects English Language Learners (ELL) and their right to a free, comprehensible education. It addresses civil and academic rights of ELL students and requires instruction be delivered in a comprehensible manner so ELLs can fully participate. Since 1975, federal law has required that students with disabilities have access to school and a free appropriate public education.

Americans with Disabilities Act of 1990 (ADA). ADA is a civil rights law that prohibits discrimination based on disability. It provides similar protections against discrimination to Americans with disabilities as the Civil Rights Act of 1964 (U.S. Department of Education, 2015).

Section 504 of the Rehabilitation Act of 1973. Section 504 regulations require a school district to provide a free appropriate public education (FAPE) to each qualified student with a disability who is in the school district's jurisdiction, regardless of the nature or severity of the disability. Under Section 504, FAPE consists of the provision of regular or special education and related aids and services designed to meet the student's individual educational needs as adequately as the needs of nondisabled students are met (U.S. Department of Education, 2015).

F. Roles and responsibilities of the special education teacher

The following has been adapted from the American Academy of Special Education Professionals and outlines the responsibilities of a special education teacher in a self-contained special education classroom in a general education school. Teachers in this role would work with a certain number of disabled students in a special education setting; however, these students also interact and learn with other nondisabled students. This type of setting allows for the use of mainstreaming or inclusion.

The teacher in a self-contained special education classroom teacher is sometimes referred to as a resource teacher and is usually supported by a teaching assistant and has the following responsibilities:

- Curriculum development

- Parent conferences

- Pre-and post-testing using group standardized tests

- Annual review-an annual meeting held by the IEP Committee to discuss the progress of each child with a disability and to plan the next year's IEP

- Involvement in the triennial evaluation process—an evaluation that takes place every three years to determine if the conditions for the original classification are still present or need to be modified.

- Monitoring the IEP, modifications, and accommodations

G. Roles and responsibilities of other professionals who deliver special education services

There are also other professionals who work with special education students. Keep in mind that these professionals do much more than what is listed here. However, the following are the main functions of each other these professionals.

- **Paraprofessional** - A special education paraprofessional, under general supervision, aids a classroom teacher, assists in the implementation of instructional programs, including self-help and behavior management.

- **Occupational Therapist** – An occupational therapist (OT) is a health care professional specializing in occupational therapy and occupational science. OTs help students strengthen their functional skills such as dressing, toileting, and eating.

- **Speech-Language Pathologist** – A speech and language pathologist (SLP) specializes in communication. SLPs work with students on speech sounds, language, social communication, voice, fluency, and feeding and swallowing.

- **School Psychologist** - School psychologists provide direct support and interventions to students, consult with teachers, families, and other school-employed mental health professionals (i.e., school counselors, school social workers) to improve support strategies, work with school administrators to improve school-wide practices and policies, and collaborate with community providers to coordinate needed services. Most often, it is the school psychologist who administers special education screening.

- **Physical Therapist** – A physical therapists assist students in accessing school environments and benefiting from their educational program by helping students with mobility, fine motor skills and gross motor skills.

> **Test Tip**
>
> You may see the term resource room or resource teacher. In a general education school, a resource room is a classroom usually found in the regular mainstream school where children with varied exceptionalities are educated at one time.

H. Collaborative approaches: strengths and limitations

Collaborative structures can be an effective way to engage students. However, they can also be a source of stress for some students. For example, students with autism spectrum disorder may get overwhelmed in a group setting. Students with behavior disorders may become aggressive or withdrawn during cooperative learning. There are several steps a teacher can take to reduce problems during collaborative actives.

Structure/routines – Set a plan in plan for when it is time to work in groups and practice the procedures for group work. Students will benefit from

Explicit instruction – Student will benefit from explicitly stated expectations. Students do not like surprises, so have a plan to communicate everything you want students to do.

Consistency – Keep group members consistent for a while. Perhaps have groups work together for an entire grading period. This will help with the routine. When it is time to change group members, clearly discuss the change and help students feel comfortable.

Roles and responsibilities – Be sure that everyone in the group is accountable for the learning taking place. This will ensure everyone is doing his or her part in the activity.

Monitor behavior – Be sure to formatively assess how your students are functioning in groups. When something is working, take note, and try to repeat it. When something causes students stress, take note, and try to eliminate it.

I. Communication with stakeholders

Stakeholders in education are people who have a stake in what is going on—students, parents, teachers, administrators, other professionals, members of the IEP team, and the community are all stakeholders. As a special education teacher, it is your responsibility to communicate effectively with stakeholders.

Parent communication – Frequent parent communication is key to building trust with parents and students. Communication should be positive. No one wants to hear all the terrible things their children do, so try to focus on strengths and opportunities for improvement. You should call parents to share milestones and happy moments. You should not call parents to vent or to be negative about students. Parent communication is most effective via phone, parent teacher conference, and email. Important information should be communicated via conference or phone. Remember, not everyone has access to email and other technology. Be sure to send information home in students home language as well.

Communication between and among other teachers/professionals – This type of communication should always be professional with the student's best interest in mind. Colleagues should discuss strategies, gains, and other school related situations with each other. Keep communication professional and remember to adhere to confidentiality standards when speaking with other professionals about students.

Communication with the IEP team – Always provide the IEP team with the necessary data, both qualitative and quantitative, to help the team make the best decisions for each student. Stay organized and focused on each student's needs and goals.

Quick Tip

Communication with stakeholders should always be positive, data-driven, and student centered. In the real world you may talk about a difficult student or parent. However, all communication should be professional.

J. Potential bias

Educators, parents, and community members may have different views about the roles that teachers, families, students, and the school play in the special educational process. It is important to reflect on your own bias and ensure it does not negatively affect students and families. Teachers who are unable to admit to their own biases often treat students and families unfairly, which obstructs students' development and families' trust in schools.

Abilities – Sometimes teachers can make assumptions about students' abilities based on their special education classification. For example, when a teacher sees that a student has ADHD, the teacher might have preconceived notions about what that means—issues with behavior, social interactions, or staying on task. However, every student is an individual and should be given a chance to be uniquely himself or herself.

Race – In many cases students of color are more likely to be labeled as having behavior problems and learning disabilities. These students are also more likely to be considered oppositional and are often assigned to remedial programs or behavioral models. It is imperative that teacher examine their own bias before making these life-changing decisions for students.

Language – Like race, language can also be a barrier for students. Often, English language learners (ELL) are labeled as having learning disabilities when they do not. In addition, assessments will often have language bias and can misrepresent a student's abilities. To combat this, teachers must provide students with ancillary materials and assessments in the student's home language. In addition, teachers must ensure that the assessments used measure skills and not language.

Quick Tip

We all have implicit and explicit bias. Being a great teacher means working to identify our own bias and ensure it is not hindering our students. Everyone makes mistakes. However, when we are aware of our own limitations, we know better and do better.

1. According to IDEA, if a special education student is expelled, the student:

    A. Loses special education services.

    B. Must appeal to the courts to continue receiving services.

    C. Continues to receive services.

    D. Is designated a case manager to determine next steps.

2. According to IDEA, special education should include:

    A. Self-contained classrooms

    B. Extracurricular activities

    C. Provide only minimal benefit.

    D. Lower standards for disabled students

3. According to IDEA, re-evaluations occur:

    A. Every three years unless both the parent and educators agree it is not necessary.

    B. Every year regardless of student progress.

    C. Every six months unless the student is making progress.

    D. In 1st, 5th, 8th and 12th grade.

4. According to IDEA, an IEP should be revised:

    A. Every 5 years

    B. Every 3 years

    C. Every 2 years

    D. Every year

5. Least restrictive environment means:

    A. Students in a wheelchair should be sat near exits.

    B. When possible special educations students should be educated with nondisabled peers.

    C. IEP teams should determine if a student can be in general education.

    D. Students should receive rewards when they achieve in the general education classroom.

6. According to IDEA, when does transition planning start?

    A. 13

    B. 14

    C. 16

    D. 18

7. Procedural safeguards have to do with:

    A. Teacher rights

    B. School rights

    C. Academic rights

    D. Parental rights

8. ADHD would fall under which of the 13 disabilities outlined in IDEA?

    A. Orthopedic impairment

    B. Intellectual disability

    C. Other health impairment

    D. Speech and language impairment

9. Which of the following is required before a student is classified as needing special education services?

    A. RTI/MTSS

    B. IEP team meeting

    C. A 504 plan

    D. Due process

10. According to MTSS, these are accommodations what most students in school receive.

    A. Tier 1

    B. Tier 2

    C. Tier 3

    D. Tier 4

Number	Answer	Explanation
1.	C	According to principle 1 of IDEA, students will receive services even if they are suspended or expelled.
2.	B	An inclusive education includes is the opportunity to participate in extracurricular activities. Therefore, answer B is the correct answer. Not all special education students require self-contained classrooms, eliminating answer A. IDEA requires MORE than minimal benefit, eliminating answer C. Lowering standards is never the correct answer, eliminating D.
3.	A	According to Principle 2, re-evaluations should occur: • When conditions warrant new information • When the parent requests re-evaluation • Every three years unless both the parent and educators agree it is not necessary
4.	D	IEPs must be revised every year with new goals.
5.	B	LRE means, whenever possible, special education students should be in general education classrooms with their peers.
6.	B	Special education students begin transition planning at 14. However, the TIP must be finished by the time the student turns 16.
7.	D	Procedural safeguards are part of Principle 6 that protect parent and student rights.
8.	C	ADHD is classified as other *health impairment*.
9.	A	RTI and MTSS are the steps teachers take before students are designated as special education. It is important that all interventions have been exhausted before a student is classified as disabled.
10.	A	Tier 1 – all Tier 2 – some Tier 3 – few Tier 4 – there is no tier 4 in MTSS.

This page intentionally left blank.

Literacy Instruction in Special Education

The following section has to do with literacy instruction. While there is no mention of literacy in the specifications for this exam, we have seen some literacy questions on the practice tests. Therefore, we wanted to be sure to add this section.

Components of Language

There are five basic components found across all languages. Language acquisition progresses across these components with increasing quantity, first with sounds then words then sentence length. The five components are described below.

Language Component	Description
Phonology	Speech structure within a language including both the patterns of basic speech units and the accepted rules of pronunciation is known as phonology. The smallest units of sounds are called **phonemes**. For example, the word "that" contains three phonemes. The "th" represents one phoneme /th/, the "a" is a short a sound /a/, and the "t" is its basic sound /t/.
Morphology	The smallest units of meanings are called **morphemes.** Morphemes include base words such as "cat," "hot," or "dove," as well as affixes such as "un-," "re-," the plural "s" or "es," and the past tense "ed." Morphology is a critical component to vocabulary development and represents the building blocks for comprehension.
Syntax	The process in which individual words and their most basic meaningful units combine to create a sentence is known as **syntax.** For example, "I went to the store" is a meaningful sentence with proper syntax while "To store went I" is not proper English.
Semantics	Semantics refers to the ways in which language coveys meaning. Semantics moves beyond literal meaning of words and is culture-dependent, which is why it is the most difficult components of language for individuals who are not native speakers or from different cultures. For example, to wish someone good luck by saying "break a leg" does not literally mean go out and break a leg.
Pragmatics	Pragmatics is the element that connects all language components and is the contextual and social use of linguistics. It focuses on the communication in language rather than structure by going beyond the literal meaning to consider how it is constructed as well as focusing on implied meaning. For example, the way we speak to our parents is different than speaking with a group of friends or the language used in a formal speech is different than the language used in a fairytale. Knowing the difference and when to use each style is pragmatics.

Characteristics of Communication Disorders

Communication disorders occur when there is an impairment in the ability to receive, send, process, and comprehend concepts or verbal, nonverbal, and graphic symbols. These disorders may be evident in hearing, language, and/or speech and range in severity from mild to profound. Whether the disorder is developmental or acquired, individuals may demonstrate one or any combination of communication disorders that result in a primary disability or secondary to other disabilities.

Speech disorder – an impairment of the articulation of speech sounds, fluency, and/or voice.

- **Articulation disorder –** atypical production of speech sounds characterized by substitutions, omissions, additions, or distortions that may interfere with intelligibility.

- **Fluency disorder –** Interruption in the flow of speaking characterized by atypical rate, rhythm, and repetitions in sounds, syllables, words, and phases. Excessive tension, struggle behavior, and secondary mannerisms are also characteristics of this disorder.

- **Voice disorder –** abnormal production and/or absences of vocal quality, pitch, loudness, resonance, and/or duration which is inappropriate for an individual's age and/or sex.

Language disorder – Impaired comprehension and/or use of spoken, written, and/or other symbol systems. This disorder may involve the form (phonology, morphology, syntax), content (semantics), and/or function (pragmatics) of language in communication in any combination.

Hearing disorder – Impaired auditory sensitivity of the physiological auditory system. This may limit the development, comprehension, production, and/or maintenance of speech and/or language. Hearing disorders are classified according to difficulties in detection, recognition, discrimination, comprehension, and perception of auditory information.

- **Deaf –** hearing disorder that limits and individual's aural/oral communication performance to the extent that the primary sensory input for communication may be other than the auditory channel.

- **Hard of hearing –** hearing disorder that is fluctuating or permanent which affects an individual's ability to communicate. Hard-of-hearing individuals rely on the auditory channel as the primary sensory input for communication.

Central Auditory Processing Disorders – deficits in the information processing of audible signals not attributed to impaired peripheral hearing sensitivity or intellectual impairment. CAPD refers to limitations in the ongoing transmission, analysis, organization, transformation, elaboration, storage, retrieval, and use of information contained in audible signals. The following are characteristics of CAPD:

- Inability to store and retrieve information efficiently

- Filter, sort, and combine information at inappropriate perceptual and conceptual levels

- Failure to attend, discriminate, and identify acoustic signals

- Inability to transform and transmit information through peripheral and central nervous systems

- Failure to attach meaning to a stream of acoustic signals through the use of linguistic and nonlinguistic contexts

(American Speech-Language-Hearing Association, 1993)

Alternate Communication and Assistive Technology

Alternate Communication

Augmentative/Alternative communication refers to any mode of communication other than speech. This includes systems such as sign language, symbol or picture boards, and electronic devices with synthesized speech. **Augmentative** systems are used by people who have some speech but are unintelligible or have limited abilities to use their speech. **Alternative** communication is when a person has no speech. There are two types of systems used to facilitate communication.

- **Unaided systems –** using your own body to include gestures, body language, facial expression, and sign language.

- **Aided systems –** using some type of tool or device and is either basic or high-tech. Pointing to pictures, letters, or words on a board is a basic system. Touching letters or pictures on a computer screen that speaks to you is high tech.

Assistive Technology

Low technology devices or systems include dry erase boards, binders, folders, albums, and other means to store or convey images or pictures used in the communication process.

Mid-technology devices or systems include tape recorders, overhead projectors, and simple voice output communication aids.

High technology devices or systems include computers, software, adaptive hardware and keyboards, and more complex voice output communication aids.

Critical Components of Reading

There are five critical components of reading.

Phonemic Awareness

Phonemic awareness is the knowledge that words are made up of a combination of individual sounds and also includes the ability to hold on to those sounds, blend them successfully into words, and take them apart again. The smallest unit of sound in a word is called a **phoneme.** For example, *cat* is made up of three phonemes (sounds) /c/ /a/ and /t/. When the three sounds are combined fluidly, they make the word *cat.* If a student knows that *cat, car,* and *cabbage* all have the same sound at the beginning of the word, then they have phonemic awareness.

Phonics

Phonics is the relationship between a specific letter and its sound as it relates to the written word. For example, a student will use phonics when faced with an unknown word while reading. By focusing on the specific sound of each letter or combination of letters, the student will break the word into pieces assigning the appropriate sound to each in order to decode the word.

Fluency

Fluency is the ability to read text accurately and smoothly with expression, intonation, and pacing to sound natural—much like speaking. Fluency depends on higher word recognition skills so that less energy is wasted on deciphering words and more is spent on comprehending what is read. The only way to improve fluency is to practice. Re-reading familiar texts several times, unison reading, modeling fluent reading, and choral reading are effective fluency strategies.

Vocabulary

Vocabulary skills increase through direct and indirect instruction. Students continuously learn new words through listening and speaking to people around them, reading on their own, and being read to by others. Some new words must be taught explicitly due to the fact they might be crucial to understanding a story or concept. It is not necessary to understand every word on a page, but too many new or difficult words hinder comprehension.

Comprehension

Comprehension is the intentional thinking process that occurs as we read. Good readers are purposeful using a variety of strategies to create meaning from text. Successful readers also monitor their comprehension by utilizing strategies when reading is understood and when it is not, use prior knowledge, make predictions, question what was read, recognize story structure, and summarize.

Quick Tip

Students with ADHD often struggle with reading comprehension because ADHD can interfere with processing information.

(National Reading Panel, 2016)

▼ **Pre-Alphabetic Phase**
Students read words by memorizing visual features or guessing words from context.

▼ **Partial-Alphabetic Phase**
Students recognize some letters and can use them to remember words by sight.

▼ **Full-Alphabetic Phase**
Readers possess extensive working knowledge of the graphophonemic system, and they can use this knowledge to analyze fully the connections between graphemes and phonemes in words. They can decode unfamiliar words and store fully analyzed sight words in memory.

▼ **Consolidated-Alphabetic Phase**
Students consolidate their knowledge of grapheme-phoneme blends into larger units that recur in different words.

Word recognition develops in the following phases: pre-alphabetic, partial-alphabetic, full-alphabetic, consolidated-alphabetic (Ehri, 1999).

Phonological awareness is the ability of the reader to recognize the sound of spoken language, including how sounds can be blended together, segmented (divided up), and manipulated (switched around).

- *Phonemic Awareness.* Understanding the individual sounds — **phonemes** — in words. For example, for a student to be able to separate the sounds in the word *cat* into three distinct **phonemes**: /k/, /æ/, and /t/.

- *Phonics/Graphophonic.* Understanding correspondence between these sounds and the spelling patterns (graphemes) that represent them. **Spelling** is phonics/graphophonics.

Deficits in Phonological Processing

Phonological disorders refer to the difficulty of understanding the sound system and speech rules of the language that normal functioning students acquire naturally. These disorders are broad in scope and more complex than simple articulation deficits.

Speech-language pathologists (SLPs) diagnose phonological disorders using standard speech assessments as well as clinical observations. The disorders are characterized as slight, mild, moderate, or severe which helps the SLP determine which therapy approaches are most effective.

A student with a phonological disorder may pronounce /s/ in *sock* clearly, but the /s/ in *bus* may be dropped and pronounced *bush*. Words with two or more syllables may be pronounced with fewer syllables—*elephant* may be pronounced *ephant*. Whole groups of sounds may be mispronounced the same way. For example, *s, f, sh,* and *ch* sounds may be pronounced as a *t, fire* becomes *tire, shoe* becomes *too,* etc.

After a diagnosis of a phonological disorder, an SLP will put together a therapy plan according to the following pattern of errors:

- Student leaves off the first or last sound in a word

- Student has difficulty producing sounds made at the back of the mouth

- Student stops sounds the should normally continue

- Student leaves off one of the sounds in a consonant blend

(Encyclopedia of Mental Disorders, 2012)

Fluent Readers

Students at this stage have fluency and prosody. **Fluency** is reading without having to stop and decode (sound out) words. Fluency involves reading a paragraph from start to finish with very few errors. **Prosody** is reading with expression while using the words and punctuation correctly. Reading with prosody means the reader is conveying what is on the page, pausing at commas and periods, and using inflection based on punctuation.

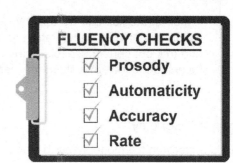

Teachers perform **fluency checks** or **fluency reads** to gauge students' reading progress. While the student reads, the teacher follows along. As the student reads, the teacher checks for **automaticity**, or how automatically the student reads. Is the student decoding too often? Can the student automatically say words as she moves down the passage? The teacher also checks the student's **accuracy** and **rate**.

Teaching strategies to increase and monitor fluency:

- *Choral Reading.* Reading aloud in unison with a whole class or group of students. Choral reading helps build students' fluency, self-confidence, and motivation.

- *Repeated Reading.* Reading passages again and again, aiming to read more words correctly per minute each time.

- *Running Records.* Following along as a student reads and marking when he or she makes a mistake or **miscues**.

- *Miscue Analysis.* Looking over the running record, analyzing why the student miscued. and employing strategies to help the student with miscues.

Quick Tip

To be considered an independent reader, a student must read at >95% accuracy.

Comprehension is the essence of reading. This is when students begin to form images in their minds as they read. They can predict what might happen next in a story because they understand what is happening in the story. Students who are in the comprehension stage of reading do not need to decode (sound out) words. They read **fluently** with **prosody**, **automaticity**, and **accuracy**.

Critical thinking is a high-level cognitive skill. This is when students can apply certain concepts to their reading. They may be able to come up with their own ending of the story or even an extra scene. This is when they are thinking deeply using evaluation and analysis in their reading.

Metacognition is thinking about thinking. When students have metacognition, they understand the processes in their minds and can employ a variety of techniques to understand text. Strategies for boosting **comprehension**, **critical thinking**, and **metacognition** are:

- *Predicting.* Asking students what they think will happen next.

- *Questioning.* Having students ask questions based on what they are reading.

- *Read aloud/think aloud.* Teacher or student reads and stops to think aloud about what the text means.

- *Summarizing.* Asking students to summarize what they just read in their own words.

Quick Tip

These strategies can be employed before, during, and after reading. For example, a teacher wants students to understand the book she is reading to the class. She stops to think aloud and talk out certain aspects of the story as she reads. She is using a *read aloud/think aloud* technique to increase students' *metacognition*, *critical thinking*, and *comprehension*.

Bloom's Taxonomy

This is a hierarchical model used to classify educational learning objectives into levels of complexity and specificity. The higher up the pyramid, the more complex the thinking skills. When answering questions regarding critical thinking, think about Bloom's Taxonomy. Below is an adaptation of Blooms Taxonomy to include more skills. On the ESE exam, you may see some skills that are not in the original Bloom's pyramid.

Think about it!

This is a Modified Bloom's Taxonomy. We Included more skills here than in the original Bloom's because you may see these skills on the exam.

Create

Analyze

Evaluate

Apply

Compare & Contrast

Categorize

Understand & Identify

Remember & Memorize

The Good Words List

My methodology is to identify what I call *good words* in the answer choices to determine correct and incorrect answers. Good words are terms and phrases taken from the test specifications that highlight best practices. If you see these words in answer choices on the exam, slow down and have a closer look. There is a good possibility these words are in the correct answer choice. I have also included a list of bad words and phrases to avoid. These are typically not the correct answer choice on the exam.

Good Words and Phrases

Accommodations. Modifying instruction or using supports to help special education students achieve. Accommodations do NOT involve lowering the standard or delaying learning.

Action research. The process of evaluating data in the classroom to identify issues and implementing effective and quick actions to solve problems.

Allocating resources. Portioning resources so all students have equal opportunity and time while balancing curriculum and instruction.

Assessments. Using formative and summative data to monitor progress and measure outcomes.

Authentic instruction. Providing students with meaningful, relevant, and useful learning experiences and activities.

Balanced literacy. Reading and writing instruction that uses a variety of literary genres including literary and informational texts.

Bilingual instruction. Helping students use elements of their first language to support learning in English.

Celebrate culture. Finding materials and resources to celebrate the different cultures represented in your classroom.

Classroom management. A variety of skills and techniques that teachers use to keep students organized, orderly, focused, attentive, on task, and academically productive during class.

Collaborative learning. These are strategies that are student-centered and self-directed rather than led by the teacher. Collaboration can also be working with colleagues or stakeholders to improve, create, or produce something.

Comprehensible education. Making information and lessons understandable to students by accommodating and using ancillary materials to help with language barriers.

Concept map. Visual representation of content. Especially useful for illustrating concepts like cause and effect, problem and solution, compare and contrast, etc.

Consent Decree. Protects students' right to a free, comprehensible education. It addresses civil and academic rights of English language learners (ELLs) and requires instruction be delivered in a comprehensible manner so all students can fully participate.

Critical thinking. Higher-order thinking skills that involve evaluating, analyzing, creating, and applying knowledge.

Cultural responsiveness. Instruction as a pedagogy that empowers students intellectually, socially, and emotionally by celebrating and learning about other cultures. This includes recognizing the importance of including students' cultural references in all aspects of learning and designing a productive learning environment.

Data driven decisions. Using scores, writing samples, observations, and other types of qualitative and quantitative data to make instructional decisions.

Depth of knowledge. Framework that is used to identify the cognitive complexity of a problem.

Developmentally appropriate instruction (DAP). Choosing text, tools, and activities that are appropriate for the students' grade level.

Differentiated instruction. Providing all learners in a diverse classroom with different methods to understand instruction.

Diversity as an asset. Seeing diversity in the classroom as an opportunity to learn new things through the perspectives of others.

Evidenced-based. Providing instruction using materials with the best scientific evidence available.

Follow the IEP. A student's individualized education program (IEP) is a legal document. If you see IEP in the answer choices, it is most likely the correct answer.

High expectations for ALL learners. Holding all students to high academic standards regardless of the students' achievement level, ethnicity, language, socioeconomic status.

Horizontal alignment. Organization and coordination of standards and learning goals across content areas in the same grade level.

Inclusive. Providing students with resources and experiences that represent their culture and ethnicity.

Informal learning. Supporting students with self-directed, collaborative learning outside of the classroom.

Interdisciplinary activities. Activities that connect two or more content areas; promotes relevance and critical thinking.

Intrinsic motivation. Answers that promote autonomy, relatedness, and competence are ways to apply intrinsic motivation. Be on the lookout for these answer choices.

Least Restrictive Environment (LRE). Educating special education students with their nondisabled peers. If you see LRE in an answer choice, it is probably the answer.

Metacognition. Analysis of your own thinking.

Modeling. Demonstrating the application of a skill or knowledge.

Modifications. Changes to the curriculum and learning environment in accordance to a student's IEP. Modifications change the expectations for learning and the level of assessment.

Outcomes. The results of a program, strategy, or resources implemented in the classroom.

Performance assessment. An activity assigned to students to assess their mastery of multiple learning goals aligned to standards.

Prior knowledge. What students know about a topic from their previous experiences and learning.

Progress monitor. Keeping track of student or whole class learning in real time. Quantifiable measures of progress, conferring, observing, exit tickets, and student self-assessments.

Relevance, real-world, and relatable. Be sure to choose answers that promote real-world application and make learning relatable to students' lives.

Reliable. Consistent. Producing consistent results under similar conditions.

Remediation. Correcting or changing something to make it better.

Rigorous. A word used to describe curriculum that is challenging and requires students to use higher-order thinking skills.

Routines/Procedures. Creating habits in the classroom helps students now what to expect every day. This type of predictability is especially helpful for students with autism spectrum disorder (ASD).

RTI/MTSS. This is a method of providing interventions before students are labeled as needing special education. If you see RTI or MTSS in an answer choice, definitely slow down and see if it fits.

Scaffolding. Using supports to help students achieve a standard that they would not achieve on their own.

Setting Clear Expectations.

This is a proactive approach to communicating how students should behave in class. This practice sets students up for success.

Specific and meaningful feedback. More than just a grade at the top of a paper, effective feedback includes positive aspects and how students can apply those positive aspects to improving. In addition, feedback should contain specific things the student should do to improve.

Standards-aligned. Ensuring that curriculum and instruction is aligned to the state-adopted standards.

Student centered/learner centered. A variety of educational programs, learning experiences, instructional approaches, and academic-support strategies that address students' distinct learning needs, interests, or cultural backgrounds.

Vertical alignment. Organization of standards and learning goals across grade levels. Structure for which learning and understanding is built from grade level to grade level.

Wait time. Time between a question and when a student is called on or a response to a student's reply.

Bad Words and Phrases

Avoid answer choices with these words or phrases.

Bias. Inserting personal beliefs, stereotypes, and assumptions in the learning process. This can also include learning materials developed from the perspective of the dominant culture that exclude minority perspectives.

Call the parents, principal, district, etc. You are expected to effectively manage your classroom without deferring responsibilities to others. In real life, teachers will often need to call the parents or principal. But on this exam, avoid answer choices that defer responsibilities to someone other than the teacher.

Exclusion. Anything that excludes a student or keeps a student away from peers is probably the wrong answer.

Extra homework. On this exam, students should be getting all of the instruction they need in class. In real life, we all assign homework. However, on this exam, extra homework is not the correct answer choice.

Hiring a contractor or external vendor. Anytime the answer choice includes using an outside resource like a contractor or a vendor to provide instruction or classroom management, this is typically not the correct answer choice. You are expected to be able to manage your own classroom using your own skills and capabilities.

Homework. Assigning homework is not a preferred strategy on this exam, especially when students are struggling with the material.

Punitive solutions. Avoid answer choices that sound like punishments. For this exam, teachers are expected to be implementing positive behavior support methods so avoid any answer choices that sounds punitive.

Student aides. While cooperative learning and social learning is very effective, stay away from answer choices where the teacher uses a student to do important work like differentiating, translating, or scaffolding for other students. Using students as translators or support for special education or ELL students can put a burden on students, which they are ill-equipped to handle.

This page intentionally left blank.

1. A special education teacher helps students keep a data folder about their classroom behaviors. In the folder are anecdotal notes about how students feel each day and how they managed their behaviors. Students rate their behaviors on a 1–5-point scale. When students get at least 15 points per week, they receive a reward. This scenario is describing:

   A. Contingency-based self-management

   B. Consequence-focused management

   C. Transitional rewards management

   D. Desensitization management

2. A special education student continually gets out of her chair to get water from the drinking fountain. This causes a disruption in the classroom. The teacher decides to move the student's seat near the water fountain and have her get up every 5 min to get a drink. The teacher sets a small timer, and when it goes off, the student is instructed to get up, and go to the fountain. She can drink if she is thirsty or stand there for 30 seconds. The student becomes tired of this and agrees to return back to class as normal and not get up to use the water fountain until designated breaks. This is an example of:

   A. Extinction

   B. Satiation

   C. Elimination

   D. Over-indulgence

3. A student in a 7th grade special education class does not want to participate in the writing activity. However, instead of expressing himself, he decides to purposely write poorly during the lesson. He also pretends to be in agreement with others in his group and the teacher. What type of behavior is this student exhibiting?

   A. ADHD

   B. Passive aggressiveness

   C. Intellectual disability

   D. Dysgraphia

4. Which of the following would be an example of manipulating the antecedent stimulus?

   A. A teacher rewards students' positive behavior with extra time on the playground.

   B. A parent tells a child that only after the child does her homework can she use electronics.

   C. A teacher builds a seating chart to prevent too much socializing during class.

   D. A teacher ignores students' bad behavior during class time.

5. A teacher is using a tally system to record the number of times a student engages in a behavior. The teacher is measuring:

   A. Latency

   B. Intensity

   C. Diversity

   D. Frequency

6. Why are social skills a main component of teaching special education?

    A. Social skills are essential in scoring well on behavioral assessments.

    B. Social skills are essential in thriving in an inclusive school environment.

    C. Social skills are more important than academic skills.

    D. The focus of general education is socialization.

7. Shelly is a special education student with emotional behavior disorder (EBD). She is consistently late to her math class. When asked about it, she tells the teacher that she has a hard time getting from one side of the building to the other before the bell rings. The teacher does not want Shelly to miss out on important instruction because of late referrals and detention. What would be the best approach in this situation?

    A. Have a conference with Shelly's parents and determine consequences for being late to class.

    B. Have the principal speak with Shelly about the importance of being on time to class.

    C. Devise a behavioral plan with Shelly that allows for 2 min of extra time for switching classes.

    D. Reward Shelly every time she is on time to class and punish her when she is late to class.

8. Which of the following are common in someone with a traumatic brain injury (TBI)? Choose all that apply.

    ☐ Appropriate response to incentive-based motivation tactics

    ☐ Inconsistent academic performance

    ☐ Deficits in critical thinking

    ☐ Inability to function appropriately in social interactions

9. What can a teacher do during direct instruction for a student who has mild hearing loss?

    A. Turn and face the student when speaking or giving instructions.

    B. Have another student write down the main points of the lesson.

    C. Ask the school for an interpreter for the student.

    D. Allow the student to record the lessons.

10. For a student to be identified as having an intellectual disability, which of the following is necessary?

    A. The student must be significantly below average in social interaction.

    B. The student must have genetic abnormalities.

    C. The student must exhibit inappropriate behavior on a regular basis.

    D. The student must have related limitations in two or more areas of adaptive skills.

11. Jerome is a 4th grade student who has ADHD. Which of the following practices would Jerome benefit from the most?

    A. Use a system of rewards and punishments.

    B. Ignore Jerome's bad behaviors.

    C. Have the principal speak to Jerome about appropriate behavior in class.

    D. Set clear expectations for classroom behavior.

12. Which of the following is most effective in identifying students who may have a learning or behavioral disability?

    A. Response to Intervention (RTI)

    B. Individualized Education Plan (IEP)

    C. Individualized Behavior Plan (IBP)

    D. Functional Behavior Assessment (FBA)

13. Julie is a 9th grade special education student in a general education culinary classroom. While she is mixing some ingredients, she becomes frustrated and throws her tools on the floor and yells profanity. Which of the following is the most appropriate way the teacher can handle the situation?

    A. Send Julie out of the room until she calms down and tell the students to continue their cooking.

    B. Talk to Julie about her behavior and come up with a plan when she gets frustrated.

    C. Call Julie's parents and ask they give Julie consequences at home.

    D. Ask that Julie's special education teacher accompany her to general education classes.

14. Jennifer is a special education student who scores on grade level in math but is significantly low in reading. Which of the following aligns with Jennifer's profile?

    A. Intellectual disability

    B. Behavior disability

    C. Specific learning disability

    D. Adaptive skills disability

15. Sam is a 10th grade student with Downs Syndrome. He enjoys school, loves to learn new things, and likes to socialize with his friends. Sam's speech and reading is at a 7th grade level. His receptive skills are on a 9th grade level. Which of the following therapies would benefit Sam the most?

    A. Occupational therapy

    B. Speech therapy

    C. Behavioral therapy

    D. Social therapy

16. Which of the following is a primary characteristic of a student with a learning disability?

    A. A discrepancy between a student's standard ability or intelligence and behavior.

    B. A discrepancy between a student's standard ability or intelligence and social skills.

    C. A discrepancy between a student's standard ability or intelligence and standardized achievement test results.

    D. A discrepancy between a student's standard ability or intelligence and adaptive skills necessary to function in the real world.

17. What is the purpose of self-monitoring?

    A. It allows students to assess and modify their own behaviors.

    B. It allows them to document negative behavior.

    C. It allows them to obtain rewards for good behavior.

    D. It allows students to imitate appropriate behavior.

18. Speech disorders are mostly associated with:

    A. Fluency

    B. Hearing loss

    C. Delay

    D. Articulation

19. Which of the following goals is appropriate for a student who has autism spectrum disorder (ASD)?

    A. Making eye contact with a partner during collaborative work.

    B. Staying seated during direct instruction.

    C. Raising a hand rather than calling out.

    D. Reading 35 words per min by the end of the year.

20. Which of the following professionals would most likely administer and intellectual assessment for a student being considered for special education?

    A. An occupational therapist

    B. A school psychologist

    C. A classroom teacher

    D. The testing coordinator

21. Sean is a 10th grade student with spina bifida with limited fine motor skills. He uses a wheelchair and has limited use of his hands and arms. He is above grade-level in reading and math. Which of the following accommodations would help Sean in social studies class?

    A. Provide Sean with fewer than normal exam questions.

    B. Seat Sean in the front of the room close to the exit.

    C. Provide Sean with copies of the presentation slides used during lecture.

    D. Provide Sean with a laptop, so Sean can type the notes.

22. Which of the following is the most effective way to plan classroom instruction for students with autism spectrum disorder (ASD)?

    A. Focus on instruction that increases academic achievement in reading and math.

    B. Focus on cooperative learning where the student has ample time to interact with peers.

    C. Focus on assessment-driven activities and help students track their progress.

    D. Focus on developing a structured environment with established routines and procedures.

23. A 10th grade general education teacher has several special education students in her science class. What is the first thing the teacher should do when planning instruction.

A. Designate appropriate accommodations.

B. Read each student's IEP.

C. Call each student's parents.

D. Conference with each student.

24. How should a special education teacher plan instruction for students who have emotional behavior disorder?

A. Design a highly organized classroom with embedded positive behavior supports.

B. Design a system of rewards and consequences that are explicitly communicated to students.

C. Design a structured cooperative learning environment where students work effectively with peers.

D. Design a plan to involve students' parents in regulating student behavior.

25. Jose is a 7th grade deaf student who is performing on grade level. Jose uses frequency modulated (FM) equipment and has an interpreter in the classroom. Which of the following would be most appropriate for Jose when he is in the computer lab working on his research paper?

A. Have the interpreter sign all cues from the computer screen.

B. Allow Jose to use a touch screen computer.

C. Have Jose use a text-to-speech screen reader.

D. Enable captions for video content.

26. What would the following statement be considered when writing a lesson plan?

Students will observe different textures of rocks and sort each of the rocks into three distinct categories: metamorphic, igneous, and sedimentary.

A. IEP goal

B. Standard

C. Objective

D. Summary

27. A special education student with intellectual disabilities who is working on functional skills would receive services from what type of professional?

A. Speech pathologist

B. Occupational therapist

C. School Psychologist

D. Physical Therapist

28. Ms. Ruiz often has her students use democratic principles for decisions made in the classroom. For example, last month, students voted on what new books to add to the classroom library and where a fish tank should be placed in the room. Using these methods regularly in the classroom help special education students with:

A. Self-advocacy

B. Self-awareness

C. Self-esteem

D. Self-control

29. Mr. Villa uses augmentative communication and assistive technology in his special education class. His instruction mainly focuses on functional curriculum. Mr. Villa most likely teaches students with:

A. Severe disabilities

B. Emotional disorders

C. ADHD

D. Specific learning disabilities

30. A teacher is planning instruction and is looking over the goals of her students with autism spectrum disorder (ASD). Which of the following would be an appropriate objective for these students during a cooperative learning activity?

A. The student will use social cues to determine when to speak.

B. The student will allow others to speak and refrain from interrupting others.

C. The student will follow instructions while working in groups.

D. The student will complete all activities during cooperative learning.

31. A teacher is planning accommodations for an upcoming standardized assessment. She has several students who have ADHD. Which of the following accommodations would be most appropriate for these students?

A. Give students extra time on the assessment.

B. Read the assessment aloud to students.

C. Allow for frequent breaks during the assessment.

D. Provide the students with large print on the assessment.

32. A 5th grade special education teacher has a student with vision impairment. Which of the following preparations should a teacher take when planning reading lessons with this student in mind?

A. Use a computer or tablet to enlarge print.

B. Allow the student to record lectures.

C. Request a paraprofessional for the student.

D. Have another student read articles and books aloud to the student.

33. A special education teacher is developing lesson plans for the following month. She will be helping students use recorders, screen readers, large keyboards, and pencil grips to access grade-level material. In her lesson plan, she would list the items under:

A. Standards

B. Assistive technology

C. Goals

D. Objectives

34. Mr. Smith is a 6th grade special education teacher with several students who have behavior disorders. Mr. Smith posts classroom expectations clearly in the front of the room, and he uses a system of rewards and consequences. Which of the following is most important to include with this approach?

A. Allow students to change the expectations when it is necessary.

B. Deliver all rewards at the end of the day so instruction is not interrupted.

C. Allow student to pick the consequences they fell are appropriate.

D. Deliver rewards frequently and immediately after student exhibit desirable behavior.

35. Which of the following would help accommodate a student with cerebral palsy?

A. Allowing the student to sit close to the teacher during lectures.

B. Providing the student with large print materials.

C. Allowing the student to record lessons and lectures.

D. Provide the student with text prediction software to take notes.

36. Parker is a special education student with autism spectrum disorder (ASD). She works with an occupational therapist on skills like feeding, toileting, and dressing. Which of the following accommodations can her special education teacher plan for when it is time for lunch and Parker is attempting to self-feed?

A. A visual step by step guide depicting the lunchroom process

B. Headphones to block out distracting noise

C. A buddy to walk through the lunch line with Parker

D. A large-handled spoon with wrist cuff

37. Ms. Jensen is working with her student, Alex, who has an intellectual disorder. Alex is in 7th grade, but he is functioning at a 3rd grade level, and he receives instruction in a resource room. Which of the following is the most appropriate goal Ms. Jensen and Alex can develop together when planning instruction for English language arts?

A. Use proper punctuation after sentences.

B. Write a 3-paragraph essay with no more than 4 errors.

C. Identify prepositional phrases in sentences.

D. Use parallel structure to write complex sentences.

38. Which of the following goals would be most appropriate for an Individualized Transition Plan (ITP) for a student who has a specific learning disability and who wants to go into graphic design after high school?

   A. Find a part-time job in a computer store.

   B. Take dual enrollment classes in using design software.

   C. Research community-living programs.

   D. Focus on real-life skills like dressing and feeding.

39. A teacher is planning a lesson and wants to be sure she is using activities that support multiple modalities. Which of the following should she consider when planning instruction?

   A. The different disabilities her students have

   B. The different learning preferences her students have

   C. The different abilities her students have

   D. The different accommodations her students need

40. Mr. Jones is planning cooperative learning activities for his 8th grade special education class. He has several students who often exhibit anxiety when presenting in a large group. For example, one of his students will not raise his hand to express himself during whole-group instruction. What should Mr. Jones' lesson plan include for these students?

   A. Plan to have these student work individually, so they do not feel anxious.

   B. Plan to have these students work with their paraprofessional only and not with the other students.

   C. Plan for a think-pair-share activity where students work with just one other student.

   D. Plan for these students to work in large groups to overcome their fears.

41. A teacher is planning functional activities for her students with intellectual disabilities. Which of the following would be the most appropriate objective in the lesson plan?

   A. Students will write a sentence in legible cursive.

   B. Students will use proper punctuation in compound complex sentences.

   C. Students will successfully memorize 50 sight words.

   D. Students will complete a job application and work with a partner to proof for errors.

42. Julien is a 4th grade student with a specific learning disability in reading. Her last assessment indicates she is reading at the beginning of 2nd grade. Which of the following goals would be most effective in helping Julien increase his fluency?

   A. On a 2nd grade non-fiction text, Julien will identify the main idea.

   B. On a 2nd grade non-fiction text, Julien will compare and contrast story elements.

   C. On a 2nd grade non-fiction text, Julien will read 100 words per min by the end of 2nd quarter.

   D. On a 2nd grade non-fiction text, Julien will sequence the events in chronological order.

43. Ms. Jacobs models appropriate behavior when engaging in cooperative activities. Which of the following foundational theories does this align?

    A. Behaviorism

    B. Cognitivism

    C. Social Learning

    D. Constructivism

44. When developing a lesson plan for the week, which of the following should a teacher consider first?

    A. Students' disabilities

    B. Students' accommodations

    C. Academic goals

    D. Academic standards

45. A teacher is planning a lesson and is making sure that the lesson reflects what was learned in the previous quarter and helps to prepare students for the following quarter. The teacher is focusing on:

    A. Vertical alignment

    B. Horizontal alignment

    C. Classroom alignment

    D. Assessment alignment

46. If a teacher wants to be sure students are exhibiting desired behaviors and skills after a lesson is over, what should be included in the lesson plan?

    A. Assessment grades

    B. Measurable objectives

    C. Literacy tests

    D. Behavior evaluations

47. An important part of any classroom that helps with stability and consistent expectations is:

    A. Setting definitive rules and consequences.

    B. Establishing routines and procedures.

    C. Communicating grades and rewards.

    D. Allowing students to decide what they learn.

48. David is a 6th grade student with a visual impairment. He is above grade level in reading and math, and he uses a resource teacher when needed in his general academic classes. In geometry class, David is working in his cooperative group to analyze geometric figures. Which of the following would be the most appropriate accommodation during this activity?

    A. Provide David with a geometric handout with large print.

    B. Provide David with manipulatives of the different 3-dimentional geometric shapes.

    C. Provide David with a buddy who can describe the different 3-dimentional geometric shapes.

    D. Provide David with a textbook with raised lines that describes geometric shapes.

Questions 49-50 refer to the following scenario.

A 3ʳᵈ grade teacher is preparing her students to welcome a new student who is blind to the class. She wants to help students understand what visual impairment is and how to support the new student.

49. The teacher wants to build empathy among the students. Which of the following activities would the teacher accomplish this?

   A. Have students read stories about famous blind people.

   B. Have students watch and listen to a video with their eyes closed.

   C. Have students go to the classroom library and choose a book while wearing a blindfold.

   D. Have students attempt to read a Braille textbook.

50. How can the teacher adapt her normal routine during direct instruction to accommodate the new student?

   A. Be sure to write all instructions clearly on the board.

   B. Ask that the student receive a helping teacher full time.

   C. Describe instructions verbally while also being explicit and clear.

   D. Have all instructions available in Braille.

51. Samantha is a 6ᵗʰ grade student with ADHD. Which of the following would be an effective way to accommodate Samantha during whole-group, direct instruction?

   A. Allow Samantha to take frequent breaks and stand in the back of the room when she needs to.

   B. Reward Samantha with extra time on the playground if she stays in her seat.

   C. Have Samantha go to the library until the whole-group activity is over.

   D. Have Samantha record the lesson and listen to it later when she can concentrate.

52. TJ is a 5ᵗʰ grade special education student in a full-inclusion classroom. This means that TJ receives services:

   A. In a general education classroom

   B. In a self-contained classroom

   C. By the school counselor

   D. By the assistant principal

53. Ms. Kaplan is working with a small group of students on their phonemic awareness. She has grouped them according to their reading level and needs. What type of grouping is Ms. Kaplan using?

   A. Flexible grouping

   B. Temporary

   C. Heterogeneous

   D. Homogeneous

54. Which of the following would be considered interactive instruction? Choose all that apply.

☐ Debates

☐ Cooperative learning

☐ Direct instruction

☐ Workshops

55. A 10th grade special education teacher is showing her students how math is not only used in the classroom, but is also used in everyday tasks like balancing checkbooks, developing budgets, completing home improvements, and cooking food. The teacher is using what type of strategy in this lesson?

A. Maintenance

B. Generalization

C. Differentiation

D. Accommodation

56. Use the chart below to determine if the method in the first column is either an intervention or an accommodation.

Activity	Intervention	Accommodation
Scaffolding instruction to help students understand a concept.	☐	☐
Providing visually impaired students screen readers.	☐	☐
Allowing for extra time on a state test.	☐	☐
Working with a small group on targeted strategies.	☐	☐

57. Which of the following represents supplementary curriculum?

A. A teacher is showing students that skills learned in school can be applied in the real world.

B. An IEP team and a student work on goal development for the upcoming school year.

C. A student uses assistive technology during lectures in general education science class.

D. A teacher uses a system of rewards and consequences to increase positive behavior.

58. Which of the following would be considered experiential learning?

A. A teacher administers a reading assessment to the class for screening purposes.

B. A student works on his homework independently after the lesson is over.

C. Special education students participate in a culinary classes bake sale.

D. Students in a special education class listen to a guest speaker on marine biology.

59. A teacher is giving explicit instructions to the whole class and modeling the task for the class before putting students in groups. The teacher is using what type of instructional approach?

A. Direct

B. Metacognitive

C. Passive

D. Multiple modality

60. Ms. Jensen is an 8ᵗʰ grade inclusion teacher who is beginning a reading lesson using a young adult novel in class. For this activity, she groups students based on reading level and provides them with different tasks based on their specific needs. Ms. Jensen is using:

A. Direct instruction

B. Whole-group instruction

C. Metacognitive instruction

D. Differentiated instruction

61. Every week students in an inclusion math class look over their data folders, chart and evaluate their progress, and develop new goals. These students are engaging in:

A. Differentiated instruction

B. Small group instruction

C. Metacognitive maintenance

D. Progress monitoring

62. After completing a lesson on dividing fractions, Mr. Ruiz had students complete a worksheet to assess their skills. After he collected the worksheet and analyzed students' answers, he realizes that 68% of the students did not fully grasp the concept of dividing fractions. What would be the most effective instructional decision Mr. Ruiz could make based on the data?

A. Reteach the concept in a different way, making sure to monitor student understanding along the way.

B. Pair students who scored low on the worksheet with those who scored high and have them work on new problems of dividing fractions.

C. Move onto the next lesson because the state test is coming up and Mr. Ruiz must cover everything in the academic plan.

D. Give students the same worksheet the following day and see if they improve after taking a break from the material.

63. A teacher is preparing for whole group instruction. She tells the students to put away their materials and sit down with their eyes up front and await further directions. When Denis finishes putting away his materials and sits down in his seat, the teacher says, "Denis, thank you so much for following instructions. You did a very good job and I appreciate that." The students hear this praise and quickly put their things away and sit down. This teacher just used:

A. Rewards and consequences

B. Positive behavior support

C. Direct feedback

D. Explicit motivation

64. Which of the following testing accommodations is most appropriate for a student with a specific learning disability (SLD) in reading?

   A. Allow the student to take the test in a private room.

   B. Allow the student to have an interpreter read the test to the student.

   C. Allow the student extra time on the exam.

   D. Allow the student to use a screen reader to read the exam aloud.

65. Which of the following accommodations is most effective for a student with traumatic brain injury (TBI)?

   A. Chunking the material into small sections.

   B. Having a resource teacher work 1-1 with the student.

   C. Pairing the student with another special education student.

   D. Allowing the student to use a laptop during lectures.

66. Which of the following would be most beneficial to a student with autism spectrum disorder (ASD) understand the class schedule?

   A. Explicit instruction outlining the schedule to the class.

   B. A partner to help the student understand the schedule.

   C. A handout with pictures the student can reference.

   D. 1-1 coaching on the steps in the schedule.

67. Which of the following is a benefit to an inclusive instructional approach?

   A. Academic achievement

   B. Proper behaviors

   C. Leadership

   D. Social skills

68. Jose is a 17-year-old student with an intellectual disability. He recently got a job at the local grocery store and will need to take the bus to and from his new job. Which of the following activities should his special education teach focus on to prepare Jose to be successful at his new job?

   A. The teacher should show Jose how to use a calculator in case he must use the register.

   B. The teacher should help Jose interpret the bus schedule, so he is on time to his new job.

   C. The teacher should show Jose how to balance his check book when he receives his paycheck.

   D. The teacher should show Jose the way to the grocery in case he misses the bus.

69. Jenny is a 7th grade special education student with dysgraphia. In her general education class, they are writing an essay. The class is working on the drafting phase first. Which of the following modifications can the teacher use to help Jenny complete this task?

   A. Have Jenny use a large grip pencil when writing the paragraph.

   B. Have another student write Jenny's paper for her.

   C. Have Jenny skip the writing assignment.

   D. Have Jenny work with a resource teacher to complete the essay.

70. A teacher is having students act out a math problem by physically getting up and moving to different sides of the room based on mathematical operations. On what type of learners in this lesson focusing?

   A. Visual

   B. Spatial

   C. Naturalistic

   D. Kinesthetic

71. Jacob is a visual learner with a behavior disorder who is assigned to a self-contained classroom. Which of the following activities would benefit Jacob most during a lesson on punctuation?

   A. Showing Jacob a video simulating how punctuation is used.

   B. Pairing Jacob with another student to do grammar exercises.

   C. Having Jacob get out of his desk and take short body movement breaks.

   D. Having Jacob complete a worksheet containing grammar exercises.

72. Which of the following is an effective way to use cooperative learning in a special education class?

   A. In groups of 5, students read and discuss text. Each student is assigned a job.

   B. In groups of 2, students complete a worksheet. Both students are responsible for finishing.

   C. In groups of 8, students read a section of a novel. Each student must read to get credit.

   D. In groups of 3, students compete in a Jeopardy game. The winning team gets candy.

73. A teacher is allowing students to complete a project either by conducting a presentation, writing an essay, creating a brochure, or making a podcast. The teacher is considering each student's:

   A. Disability

   B. Accommodations

   C. Learning preferences

   D. IEP

74. A special education teacher is working with severely disabled students on how to feed themselves, dress themselves, and engage in other life skills. Which of the following professionals can assist this teacher with this type of instruction?

   A. School counselor

   B. Occupational therapist

   C. Physical therapist

   D. Assistant principal

75. Sarah is a 3rd grade student who is struggling academically and who has become defiant. She refuses to do her work in class and often acts inappropriately. Her parents want her tested for a learning disability. Which of the following professionals is most likely to evaluate Sarah?

   A. Occupational Therapist

   B. School psychologist

   C. Classroom teacher

   D. School counselor

76. A general education math teacher creates a timed assessment on multiplication. The quiz is 10 questions in 10 min. The teacher is looking for students to score at 90% accuracy. A special education student takes the assessment and gets two correct, six incorrect, and leaves two unanswered. What should be the next step in helping the student?

   A. Reteach the material and allow the student to retake the test without being timed.

   B. Assign the same assignment again to the student until he reaches the desired outcome.

   C. Assign extra multiplication homework to remediate the student's skills.

   D. Have a paraprofessional work one-on-one with the student and allow for a retake.

77. After a student submits her test and it is graded by the computer, the teacher sees a raw score of 78. What does this mean?

   A. The student scored 78%.

   B. The student is in the 78th percentile.

   C. The student answered 78 questions correctly.

   D. The student's scale score is 78.

78. A cognitive assessment is most appropriate in measuring:

   A. Behavior

   B. Functional skills

   C. Social skills

   D. Intellectual ability

79. The Vineland Adaptive Behavior Scale is used to measure:

   A. Physical ability in the real world

   B. Life skills and intellectual ability

   C. The extent of a student's disability

   D. Student behavior in academic settings

80. Which of the following is the most appropriate way to use a summative assessment?

   A. To assign students a percentile ranking

   B. To use as an ongoing measure of students' abilities

   C. To measure student work samples over a period

   D. To measure outcomes after a teacher finishes a unit

81. Which of the following is the primary purpose of a formative assessment?

   A. To progress monitor

   B. To rank students

   C. To measure outcomes

   D. To collect work samples

82. For a student to be classified as having a severe intellectual disability, the student has to score at what level on the Wechsler Intelligence Scale for Children (WISC) or IQ test.

A. Below 120

B. Below 90

C. Below 70

D. Below 30

83. A special education student is taking the Woodcock-Johnson Psycho-Educational Battery, Third Edition. What is this assessment measuring?

A. A learning disability

B. An intellectual disability

C. Social skills

D. Life skills

84. Julie is a 3rd grade student who is having trouble keeping up in the classroom, especially during reading and math time. Julie's parents spoke with the teacher and want to see if Julie has a learning disability. What is the first step the teacher should take?

A. Formally test the student using Vineland Adaptive Behavior Scale.

B. Have the school psychologist come in and observe Julie in reading and math.

C. Recommend the parents meet with the principal to see if special education is an option.

D. Reduce the amount of reading and math tasks Julie is required to complete in class.

85. Sam has ADHD and a specific learning disability in reading. What would be the most appropriate accommodations to provide Sam during a state standardized assessment? Choose all that apply.

☐ Have the proctor read the assessment aloud to Sam.

☐ Allow Sam to take frequent breaks.

☐ Allow Sam to have extra time to take the assessment.

☐ Break the assessment up over several days.

86. Which of the following behaviors might be outlined on a functional behavior assessment (FBA)?

A. James frequently struggles to remember his multiplication facts.

B. James has trouble eating with utensils and drinking out of a standard drinking glass.

C. James can finish his assignments when he is given extra time.

D. James frequently uses profanity and pushes other students when it's time to line up.

87. An example of proper use of a criterion-referenced exam in an English language arts class would be to:

A. Rank students by percentile

B. Use in a rubric to evaluate skills

C. Screen students for class placement

D. Measure students' mastery of the standards

88. Which of the following would be the most appropriate testing accommodation for a Juan, who is on grade-level but has limited use of his hands?

    A. Provide Juan with large print on assessments.

    B. Provide Juan with a screen reader for assessments.

    C. Allow Juan to respond orally to assessment questions.

    D. Allow Juan to have extra time on the assessment.

89. This type of assessment usually provides a score report with scale scores, percentile ranking, and ability levels.

    A. State standardized test

    B. Rubric

    C. Formative assessment

    D. Informal assessment

90. A special education teacher wants to collect student writing samples over a semester and have students analyze their performance from the beginning of the semester to the end of the semester. This type of assessment is a:

    A. Performance-based assessment

    B. Portfolio assessment

    C. Norm-referenced assessment

    D. Ongoing assessment

91. Which of the following provides rich qualitative data regarding student behavior a teacher can use to provide interventions?

    A. Diagnostic assessment

    B. Student survey

    C. Anecdotal record

    D. Oral assessment

92. Ms. Jones is working with her special education students using a new reading program adopted by the district. Which of the following pair of assessments would be most beneficial when measuring the effectiveness of a new reading program?

    A. Pretest and summative

    B. Pretest and formative

    C. Diagnostic and norm-referenced

    D. Screening and formative

93. A teacher is analyzing a student's behavior after several intervention strategies. She wants to figure out which intervention diminishes the negative behavior. What can the teacher determine based on the data presented in the graphs below.

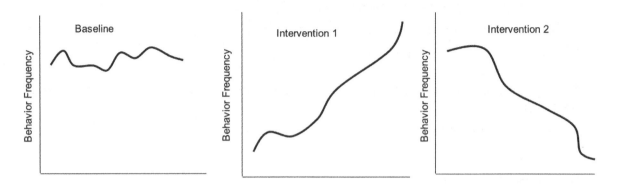

A. A new diagnostic test will need to be administered better baseline data.

B. Intervention 1 is more effective than intervention 2.

C. Intervention 2 is more effective than intervention 1.

D. Neither intervention 1 or intervention 2 was effective.

94. Which of the following is an example of a teacher using data to drive instructional decisions in the classroom?

A. A teacher is walking around the room and observing students working on math problems.

B. A teacher conferences with students to discuss feedback of their writing.

C. A teacher uses reading scores to group students temporarily for interventions.

D. A teacher is planning a performance-based assessment.

95. One of the skills outlined in a student's IEP is to participate in group situations actively and appropriately. A teacher has the student actively participate in a cooperative learning exercise. She observes and records the student's efforts in contributing to the group discussion, waiting her turn to speak, and sharing relevant information to the discussion. This assessment is:

A. Problem based

B. Performance based

C. Project base

D. Standards based

96. This test evaluates three areas: participation, task support, and activity performance.

A. Behavior Assessment System for Children (BASC)

B. School Function Assessment (SFA)

C. Woodcock-Johnson Psycho-Educational Battery, Third Edition

D. Vineland Adaptive Behavior Scale

97. Which of the following would be considered a procedural safeguard under IDEA?

    A. Parents have the right to be involved with decisions made in an IEP meeting.

    B. Special education students must be educated in the least restrictive environment.

    C. All special education students are to receive a free appropriate public education (FAPE)

    D. A student's IEP must be reviewed every year.

98. According to Section 504 of the Rehabilitation Act, a student who needs related services but does not qualify for special education:

    A. Cannot receive services

    B. Must pay for services

    C. Must prove they have a disability

    D. Is entitled to services

99. Which of the following is an essential component of an IEP?

    A. Accommodations

    B. Measurable goals

    C. Parent signatures

    D. Teacher involvement

100. Ms. Jackson, a resource teacher, is preparing her handouts for open house. She knows that under IDEA, parents should be involved in the educational decision-making process. Which of the following information should she be prepared to collect from parents during open house?

    A. Primary guardian status

    B. Parent contact information

    C. Names of siblings in special education

    D. Parent work status

101. Jane is a 7th grade special education student. The IEP team wants to make minor changes to her IEP. Under the procedural safeguards provision in IDEA, what is the team required to do?

    A. Allow the student to approve the changes.

    B. Ask for supporting data from the teacher.

    C. Consult with the school psychologist.

    D. Notify parents of any changes.

102. The Individuals with Disabilities Education Act (IDEA) is a:

    A. State law that protects special education students from discrimination.

    B. State law that ensures all students receive accommodations.

    C. Federal law that requires parents of students with disabilities to pay for special services.

    D. Federal law that ensures all students with disabilities receive a free appropriate public education

103. An IEP that outlines goals and objectives that align to the general academic curriculum and state benchmarks is referred to as a:

A. Transition IEP

B. Family-based IEP

C. Standards-based IEP

D. Student-centered IEP

104. Under Part B of IDEA students can receive public education services until they are:

A. 3-16

B. 3-18

C. 3-21

D. 3-30

105. Raúl is a special education student who has a behavior disorder. The school decided to move Raúl from general education to a self-contained classroom. Raúl's parents do not agree with this decision. What can the parents do?

A. Request a due process hearing.

B. Request he be switched to a private school.

C. Request the superintendent reprimand the administration.

D. Request the records of students in the self-contained classroom.

106. According to IDEA, federal safeguards are required for which of the following? Choose all that apply.

☐ Initial evaluation

☐ Reevaluation

☐ Revision of annual goals

☐ Formative assessment

107. Which of the following is listed as one of the 13 disabilities according to IDEA?

A. ADHD

B. Visual impairment

C. Cerebral palsy

D. Down Syndrome

108. Students with disabilities receive at least one annual review of their IEP, are guaranteed due process rights, and are entitled to keeping their records confidential under what federal law?

A. FAPE

B. IDEA

C. LRE

D. FERPA

109. Which of the following shows the least restrictive environment (LRE) to the most restrictive environment?

    A. A special education student is in a self-contained special education classroom, a special education student is participating in culinary class and then goes back to the special education classroom, a special education student is in a general education classroom and receives services when needed.

    B. A special education student is in a self-contained special education classroom, a special education student is in a general education classroom and receives services when needed, a special education student is participating in culinary class and then goes back to the special education classroom.

    C. A special education student is participating in culinary class and then goes back to the special education classroom, a special education student is in a self-contained special education classroom, a special education student is in a general education classroom and receives services when needed.

    D. A special education student is in a general education classroom and receives services when needed, a special education student is participating in culinary class and then goes back to the special education classroom, a special education student is in a self-contained special education classroom.

110. A copy of procedural safeguards must be provided to the parents/guardians of an exceptional student in all of the following situations EXCEPT:

    A. When a change in placement occurs because of a discipline procedure.

    B. When requesting for an evaluation into exceptional student education.

    C. First due process hearing of the school year.

    D. Parent/teacher conference to discuss academics

111. A teacher notices one of her special education students is not achieving on her math exams. When she looks over the IEP, she sees that one of the goals outlined in the student's IEP is to meet math proficiency at 80%. She determines this goal is too high for the student. She decides to change the goal on the IEP to be more realistic of the student's abilities. What did this teacher fail to consider?

    A. The rights of parents to participate in the decision-making process of the IEP.

    B. The credibility of the IEP team in its ability to make appropriate goals for the student.

    C. The safety of the learning environment.

    D. The quality of instruction.

112. Local public schools must provide services designed to help special education students meet their annual goals and make progress in the general curriculum at no cost to the parent. This is:

    A. Least Restrictive Environment (LRE)

    B. Procedural Safeguards

    C. Appropriate Evaluation

    D. Free Appropriate Public Education (FAPE)

113. A college student is conducting a case study for a master's program in special education. The college student reaches out to a special education teacher for help with the case study. The college student is requesting records of special education students in the school. What should the special education teacher do?

A. Provide the college student with the records after her identity has been verified.

B. Provide the records only after documentation has been signed before giving out the records.

C. Ask the principal to speak with the college student and determine if the records can be given out.

D. Refuse the college student's request for records on the grounds of FERPA.

114. Why is there a disproportionate over-representation of English Language Learners (ELLs) in special education?

A. Cultural and language bias

B. High expectations

C. Low expectations

D. Lack of experienced teachers

115. A special education student's parents do not speak. What should the IEP team do to make sure the parents are actively involved in the IEP process as protected by IDEA?

A. Provide all written materials in the parents' native language and require the parents to provide their own translator.

B. Provide a translator for the meeting and provide the parents with all meeting materials in their native language.

C. Allow the student to translate the meeting and materials to the parents.

D. Hold the meeting with the parents, allow parents to ask the staffing specialist questions.

116. Which of the following would NOT be included in the IEP?

A. Peer interaction data

B. Classroom accommodations

C. Measurable goals and objectives

D. Least restrictive environment

117. During the evaluation process, when is a Present Levels of Academic Achievement and Functional Performance (PLAAFP) administered?

A. Initial evaluation

B. Reevaluation

C. Revision of goals

D. Accommodations evaluation

118. Before referring a student to special education, which of the following is essential in making sure the student is being identified properly?

   A. Conference with the student and document qualitative data.

   B. Talk with the principal and school psychologist to gain multiple perspectives.

   C. Provide and document intensive supports and interventions such as RTI or MTSS.

   D. Conference with the parents to be sure they approve of the designation.

119. Under IDEA, school districts must provide which of the following to all special education students?

   A. Modified curriculum

   B. Preferred accommodations

   C. Extended school year provisions

   D. Education in the least restrictive environment.

120. According to IDEA, at what age can a student begin the transition IEP process?

   A. 12

   B. 14

   C. 16

   D. 18

This page intentionally left blank.

Number	Answer	Category	Explanation
1	A	I.	Contingency-based self-management makes students responsible for managing their own behavior and rewards them for appropriate behavior.
2	B	I.	Satiation is a technique teachers use to overindulge a negative behavior so much that the student becomes bored with the bad behavior and stops doing it.
3	B	I.	Passive-aggressive behavior is a deliberate, but covert way of expressing feelings of anger (Long, Long & Whitson, 2009). Passive aggression is motivated by a young person's fear of expressing anger directly.
4	C	I.	Removing the antecedent stimulus is a type of intervention that changes students' behavior by manipulating conditions that *precede* such behavior. Constructing a seating chart before the behavior happens is an example of this.
5	D	I.	The key words here are *the number of times the behavior happens.* This indicates frequency.
6	B	I.	The goal is inclusion. Therefore, social skills are key to an inclusive school experience for a special education student.
7	C	I.	The best choice in this situation is one that uses good words and practices. Devising a behavioral plan with Shelly is best practice because it allows Shelly to take ownership of her situation. In addition, because she has an IEP, accommodating her to give her extra time is also appropriate. All of the other answer choices are punitive in nature and are not appropriate.
8	Boxes 2, 3 & 4	I.	Students with TBI can experience an array of complex problems, including inconsistencies in academic performance, inappropriate responses in social situations, and deficits in problem solving and abstract thinking. Box 1 is not correct because students with TBI often do not respond to incentives.
9	A	I.	With mild hearing loss, it helps for a student to see the teacher's lips when the teacher is speaking. Therefore, being sure to face the class when speaking will help students with mild hearing loss understand what is being said. All of the other options are not appropriate for this scenario.

Number	Answer	Category	Explanation
10	D	I.	Adaptive skills are defined as practical, everyday skills needed to function and meet the demands of one's environment, including the skills necessary to effectively and independently take care of oneself and to interact with other people. This is the only answer choice that addresses intellectual skills. Answers A and C all deal with social or behavioral skills. Answer B does not necessarily affect intellectual ability. For example, a student could have a genetic disfunction like Sickle Cell Anemia and still perform in academics and in adaptive skills.
11	D	I.	Setting clear expectations is always the first best approach to any classroom situation. When students know exactly what is expected of them, they are more likely to meet those expectations. The question asks for the practice Jerome would benefit from *most*. Therefore, answer D is correct. Also setting clear expectations is on the Good Words list.
12	A	I.	Response to intervention (RTI) is a system designed to identify students at risk for poor academic and behavioral outcomes, so the school can develop strategies to help the students succeed. An IEP and BEP are used after a student is identified, and a functional behavior assessment is a measure of a student's functional skills. **NOTE**: RTI is sometimes referred to as MTSS—multi-tiered system of supports.
13	B	I.	In this situation, the most effective thing to do is speak with Julie about her behavior and see if the teacher and Julie can come up with a plan to manage the behavior. The goal is to keep Julie in general education. One outburst should not jeopardize that. Remember, punitive measures are usually not the correct answer on the exam.
14	C	I.	Because Jennifer struggles with a specific academic area, she has a specific learning disability. None of the other choices fit Jennifer's profile.
15	B	I.	Because Sam struggles most with speech and reading, speech therapy would be the most appropriate here. Occupational therapy works on everyday skills needed to operate in the real-world. Behavioral therapy is most appropriate for those who struggle with behavioral disorders. Social therapy is used for people who have a hard time managing social anxiety.
16	C	I.	The primary indicator that a student is struggling with a learning disability is when there is a discrepancy between test scores and ability.
17	A	I.	Self-monitoring is effective because it empowers students to regulate and modify their own behavior. Answers B, C, and D focus on rewards or negative consequences. Answer A is the best choice.

Number	Answer	Category	Explanation
18	D	I.	An articulation disorder is characterized by difficulty in pronouncing certain sounds correctly, most commonly the R sound and the S sound. This is the most common aspect of speech disorders.
19	A	I.	ASD is characterized by inadequate social skills. Therefore, answer A is the most effective goal for the student in this situation.
20	B	I.	A school psychologist usually conducts assessments that measure a student's intellectual abilities. An occupational therapist works with students on functional skills. The classroom teacher and the testing coordinator are not qualified for this task.
21	C	II.	The key information here is that Sean is above grade level in his academics. Therefore, we want to accommodate Sean without reducing rigor. Providing Sean with the slides from the lecture is the best answer because it accommodates Sean but keeps rigor high. Answer choice A is not effective here because reducing the number of questions on the exam reduces rigor. Sitting Sean in the front of the room does nothing to help him in this situation. Finally, if Sean has limited use of his arms and hands, access to a laptop if useless in this situation.
22	D	II.	Students with autism spectrum disorder (ASD) need a highly structured environment with predictable routines to minimize disruptive and distractive behaviors. Also, the words routines and procedures are on the Good Words list for this exam.
23	B	II.	The very first thing any teacher who has special education students in class should do is read the students' IEPs.
24	A	II.	While all of the answer choices may seem reasonable for this question, the only effective practice is outlined in answer A. Students with emotional behavior disorders (EBD) benefit from a structured learning environment. In addition, positive behavior support is essential when working with students with EBD. This will help students improve their behavior with intrinsic supports. Answer B is not the most effective because it focuses on rewards and consequences which are extrinsic motivators. Answer C cannot be attained until students can regulate their behavior. Finally, answer D is ineffective because calling students' parents is outside of the classroom. It is the special education teacher's job to help students in the classroom. Calling home for help is usually the incorrect answer.

Number	Answer	Category	Explanation
25	D	II.	Enabling visual cues such as captions for video content allows Jose to see when auditory elements occur. Having Jose's interpreter sign every single cue on the computer is impossible and unnecessary. He is deaf but can still read the screen, so a screen reader is not going to help him. A touch screen is not helpful here because Jose has use of his hands.
26	C	II.	Objectives are the observable behaviors or skills students will exhibit during a lesson. Objectives usually start with, "the students will…"
27	B	II.	Occupational therapists help students learn skills that will help them in the real world or everyday activities (functional skills).
28	C	II.	Students feel empowered when they are part of the decision-making process; therefore, self-esteem is the correct answer. Self-advocacy, self- awareness, and self-control are not appropriate here because those skills are often associated with individual behaviors. This scenario is a group decision-making process.
29	A	II.	Augmentative communication, assistive technology and functional curriculum is associated with students who have severe disabilities.
30	A	II.	Autism spectrum disorder (ASD) is characterized by poor social interactions, so an objective that focuses on social cues is most appropriate for this scenario.
31	C	II.	Attention-deficit/hyperactivity disorder (ADHD) is characterized by difficulty focusing, and frequent breaks are an accommodation for students who cannot concentrate for long periods of time.
32	A	II.	Enlarging print is the most appropriate because the student is visually impaired.
33	B	II.	These are all examples of assistive technology that allows students to access the curriculum.
34	D	II.	Rewards for positive behavior are very effective for students with behavior disabilities; therefore, answer D is the best answer. Focusing on the positive and delivering rewards immediately helps to reinforce positive behaviors.
35	D	II.	Students with cerebral palsy often have difficulty writing because they have limited use of their hands, so using a computer with word-prediction software will allow the student to be independent and take notes.
36	D	II.	According to the scenario, Parker has trouble with fine motor skills because she needs help dressing, toileting, and feeding. Therefore, the best accommodation for this situation is a large-handled spoon with wrist strap.

Praxis Special Education

Number	Answer	Category	Explanation
37	A	II.	According to the scenario, Alex is functioning at a 3rd grade level. The only developmentally appropriate activity listed for that level is using punctuation properly. The other answer choices outline skills above a 3rd grade level.
38	B	II.	This student should be focusing on postsecondary education. While she has a specific learning disability, she can receive accommodations for that disability in college. Since her interest is in graphic design, she should be transitioning toward postsecondary education that will get her a degree or certification in that area. None of the other answer choices are appropriate for this student.
39	B	II.	Multiple modalities have to do with learning preferences. This is sometimes referred to as multiple intelligences. This is when the teacher plans for activities that are beneficial for visual, auditory, kinesthetic and read/write learners.
40	C	II.	Think-pair-share is a 1-1 cooperative learning activity where students share their ideas or learning with another student. It is important that the teacher help the student participate in activities in class. Therefore, having the student work individually or just with a paraprofessional are not effective approaches here. Also, forcing a student to work in a big group to "overcome his fears" may be too much too soon and cause the student more anxiety. A think-pair-share activity is an effective way to have students work with just one other student and begin to feel comfortable sharing ideas.
41	D	II.	Functional curriculum is used to help students with life skills. The only life skill listed in the answer choices is filling out a job application.
42	C	II.	Fluency is defined as the ability to read with speed, accuracy, and proper expression. Therefore, answer choice C is the most effective. See the *Teaching Literacy in Special Education* section of the book for more information on these specific skills.
43	C	II.	A. **Behaviorism** studies student behavior as a response to stimuli (rewards and consequences). B. **Cognitivism** focuses on intellectual growth and how students learn C. **Social Learning** asserts that new behaviors can be acquired by observing and imitating others. D. **Constructivism** says learning is a result of your experiences and what you bring to the learning.
44	D	II.	Standards should always be the FIRST thing a teacher references when developing a lesson plan. Students' disabilities, accommodations, and goals are all important. However, standards come first.

Number	Answer	Category	Explanation
45	A	II.	Vertical alignment occurs then one skill or grade level builds to the next. Horizontal alignment is when content areas are aligned. For example, when a science lesson incorporates math and English skills. Answers C and D are nonsense answers.
46	B	II.	Learning objectives are the behaviors or skills students are expected to acquire in a lesson. These objectives should be measurable, meaning teachers should be able to determine if the objective is met either by a formative or summative assessment.
47	B	II.	Routines and procedures are on the Good Words list. Therefore, if you see them in an answer choice, it is probability the correct answer. Beyond that, routines and procedures help students understand exactly what is expected every day. In addition, routines provide all students, not just special education students, with stability they crave in the learning environment. Students like routines and procedures. They do not like instability and uncertainty.
48	B	III.	Not only will manipulatives help David analyze different shapes, this is also a way to bring the abstract to real life. In fact, the manipulatives would help the other students too. Larger print and raised print do help visually impaired students. However, those options are not as beneficial as holding and feeling geometric shapes. Having a buddy describe the shapes is not appropriate here.
49	C	III.	All of these activities would be beneficial in getting students to understand what it is like to be blind. However, the best activity would be to try to find the classroom library and pick a book blindfolded. This will help build empathy because students will see how an activity, one they engage in every day, can become much more complicated when they simulate being visually impaired.
50	C	III.	Because the student is visually impaired, using a clear concise manner to verbally describe instructions is the best answer. Writing the instructions on the board does little to help a student who is blind. In addition, asking for a helping teacher full time is unrealistic. Finally providing all notes in Braille is probably not possible. Answer C is the best accommodation because it can be achieved with minor changes in the teacher's instructional approach.
51	A	III.	Students with ADHD often need to take breaks. Answer choice A is the most appropriate because it keeps Samantha in the activity, but it also allows her to get up when she needs to.
52	A	III.	Full inclusion means that TJ is in regular classes and his teachers accommodate him in the general classroom. This is the least restrictive environment for TJ.

Number	Answer	Category	Explanation
53	D	III.	When a teacher groups students together who have the same skill level or who have the same needs, the teacher is using homogenous grouping. The word *homo* means *the same*.
54	Boxes 1, 2 & 4	III.	The only activity listed that is not interactive instruction is box 3. Direct instruction is when the teacher stands in the front of the room and lectures. The students are passive participants, not active participants. Yes, student can raise their hands and ask questions or make statements, but direct instruction is not considered interactive instruction.
55	B	III.	Generalization strategies are those that help students perform a skill in a variety of settings. This is sometimes referred to as transfer because students can transfer the skill to one activity to another.

For question 56:

Activity	Intervention	Accommodation
Scaffolding instruction to help students understand a concept.	☑	☐
Providing visually impaired students screen readers.	☐	☑
Allowing for extra time on a state test.	☐	☑
Working with a small group on targeted strategies.	☑	☐

Number	Answer	Category	Explanation
56	See explanation	III.	Interventions are used for special education and general education students to meet the needs of every student. Accommodations are formal changes that remove barriers base on a student's disability.
57	C	III.	Supplementary curriculum and aids are services and other supports that are provided in regular education classes, other education-related settings, and in extracurricular and nonacademic settings, to enable children with disabilities to be educated with nondisabled children to the maximum extent appropriate.

PRACTICE TEST

Number	Answer	Category	Explanation
58	C	III.	Experiential learning is learning by doing. Students who are participating in a culinary bake sale are doing the task rather than reading about the task or learning about the task. Therefore, answer C is the best answer. You may be tempted to pick a guest speaker, answer D. However, a guest speaker is simply a lecture. Students are sitting and listening.
59	A	III.	When the teacher is doing the work in the front of the room, like the scenario in the question, the teacher is using direct instruction. A metacognitive approach is helping students think about their thinking. Passive instruction is not a real thing. Finally, a multiple modality approach is paying attention to learning preferences by using visual, auditory, kinesthetic, and other techniques based on multiple intelligences.
60	D	III.	The key phrase in the question is *provides them with different tasks based on their specific needs.* That is differentiated instruction. To differentiate is to modify activates based on students' abilities or needs. That is what the teacher is doing in this scenario.
61	D	III.	Teachers and students progress monitor by continuously looking at data, both qualitative and quantitative, to measure academic improvement. This practice is outlined in the example scenario.
62	A	III.	Because such a high percentage of students did not understand the lesson as indicated by the worksheet data, the teacher must reteach the lesson. That is the only appropriate answer here. Partnering students up sounds like a good idea. However, when students are lacking the skill at that magnitude, having them work with a partner puts the burden of differentiation on the student who is not trained as a teacher. it is best to reteach the lesson in this scenario.
63	B	III.	The teacher is focusing on the positive behavior Denis displayed and praises him for it. This not only helps to reinforce the behavior in Denis, but it also helps to reinforce the behavior in his peers.
64	C	III.	Students with SLD usually receive extra time on the exams. None of the other answer choices are appropriate for this student's disability.
65	A	III.	Students with this TBI may have memory problems, difficulty paying attention, impulsiveness, poor organizational skills, and difficulty reasoning abstractly. Therefore, chunking the material into small sections is most appropriate for this student.
66	C	III.	Students with ASD often do better when things are represented with pictures than with direct instruction and cooperative learning. One-to-one academic coaching on the schedule is not appropriate here. There is not time to do this every time there is a schedule change. A handout is most convenient and most effective for this scenario.

Praxis Special Education

Number	Answer	Category	Explanation
67	D	III.	Because the goal of special education is to prepare students for the real word, social skills are just as important as academic skills. Usually on the exam, inclusion is associated with social skills.
68	B	III.	It is important that Jose understand the transportation schedule, so he can be on time to his job. None of the other answer choices are as important than that. This is a functional skill the teacher must focus on to help Jose be successful in the real world.
69	A	III.	Dysgraphia affects a person's handwriting ability and fine motor skills. Therefore, allowing Jenny to use a large grip pencil will help her with this task.
70	D	III.	Body movements are kinesthetic movements and that is what this scenario is focusing on.
71	A	III.	Because Jacob is a visual learner, a video is the best fit for this scenario.
72	A	III.	The most effective way to use cooperative learning is to have no more than 5 members, eliminating answer C, where each student has a job and completes a learning activity. Answer A is the only choice that outlines this.
73	C	III.	This method is allowing students to choose from different learning preferences to complete a task. This is not an accommodation. Rather, this is a way to differentiate based on multiple intelligences or learning preferences.
74	B	III.	Occupational therapists work with students on life skills like the ones mentioned in this scenario. None of the other professionals are qualified for these tasks.
75	B	IV.	School psychologists conduct cognitive assessments that measure a student's intellectual abilities. They are usually the first professionals to evaluate students for special education.
76	A	IV.	The student needs more support because of the low score. However, the student also did not answer 2 of the questions indicating that the student ran out of time. To accurately measure this student's skills, reteaching the material and allowing for the test to be untimed is most appropriate in this situation.
77	C	IV.	A raw score measures how many questions the test taker got correct. You may be tempted to choose answer A. However, we do not know how many total questions there are so 78% cannot be the answer. If there were 100 questions, then the raw score and percentage would be 78. However, this student could have scored a 78/80, which is 98% or a 78/120, which is 65%.

Number	Answer	Category	Explanation
78	D	IV.	Cognitive means intellectual or having to do with the brain. A common cognitive assessment is an intellectual quotient (IQ) test.
79	B	IV.	Intellectual ability is not just a measure of how a person scores on an academic assessment. Intellectual ability has to do with life skills, social concerns, social skills, and ability. The Vineland Adaptive Behavior Scale test measures intellectual ability in these areas.
80	D	IV.	Summative assessments happen at the end of learning and measure outcomes. Answer A describes a norm-referenced assessment. Answer B describes a formative assessment. Answer C describes a portfolio (also considered formative) assessment.
81	A	IV.	Formative assessments are ongoing and help a teacher to measure progress and adjust instruction when needed.
82	C	IV.	Below 70 on an IQ test is considered having a severe intellectual disability.
83	A	IV.	The Woodcock-Johnson Psycho-Educational Battery, Third Edition provides a comprehensive set of individually administered tests to measure cognitive abilities, scholastic aptitudes, and achievement. It is important to remember, an intellectual disability and learning disability are two different conditions.
84	B	IV.	Because it is early, observation by the school psychologist is the best first step. Formal testing outlined in answer A is jumping ahead. Answer C, meeting with the principal, is not appropriate. Finally, simply reducing the amount of reading and math tasks is not effective in this situation.
85	Boxes 2, 3, & 4	IV.	These three accommodations are appropriate for Sam's situation. However, on a state assessment, those accommodations must be listed on the IEP. Teachers cannot just provide accommodations on a state test as they see fit. Reading the test aloud to Sam does nothing to help him considering his disabilities.
86	D	IV.	A functional behavior assessment (FBA) is a process for identifying problem behaviors and developing interventions to improve or eliminate those behaviors. You may be tempted to choose answer B. However, answer B aligns with a functional skills assessment. This scenario is a functional behavior assessment.
87	D	IV.	Criterion-referenced exams measure students' knowledge against a criterion. The most common and arguably important criteria is the state standards. State standardized assessments are considered criterion-referenced tests.

Number	Answer	Category	Explanation
88	C	IV.	The best accommodation for this situation is to allow Juan to respond orally; this way he can demonstrate his learning without having to use his hands to write. Juan does not need large print or a screen reader because he not visually impaired. Also, Juan is on-grade level, so he does not need extra time, eliminate answer D.
89	A	IV.	A state-standardized test is a formal assessment that usually provides data on scale scores, achievement levels and percentile ranking. Even if you do not know a lot about scale scores or percentile rankings, you can use process of elimination to get the correct answer. The elements described in the question are formal, so we can eliminate answer D immediately. A rubric is used to grade essay writing or projects and does not fit here, eliminating answer B. Finally, a formative assessment is a type of informal check like an observation or a quick assessment, so we can eliminate that.
90	B	IV.	Because the teacher is collecting specific student artifacts over time, this is a portfolio assessment.
91	C	IV.	For student behavior, observations with anecdotal notes is most effective. The anecdotes provide context and description off the student's behavior. All other answer choices do not address student behavior, rather they address student learning.
92	A	IV.	Summative data measures progress when the lesson, strategy, or unit is finished. Determining the effectiveness of a reading program requires student scores at the beginning (pretest) and at the end after the reading program was administered (post-test or summative). Formative assessments are ongoing, during the teaching, so formative assessments would not be helpful in evaluating the effectiveness of a program. Therefore, answer choices B and D are not appropriate in this situation. A norm-referenced test does not give specific information about skills learned, so answer choice C also does not fit this situation.
93	C	IV.	In this case, the frequency of behavior goes up with intervention 1. The frequency of behavior goes down with intervention 2. Therefore, intervention 2 is more effective than intervention 1.
94	C	IV.	In every answer choice the teacher is administering an assessment of some kind. However, only in answer choice C does she make a decision—grouping and interventions.
95	B	IV.	A performance-based assessment measures a student's ability to apply knowledge or skills to perform a task in a relevant situation. In this case, the student is using appropriate behavior in a group setting. Answer choice B is the best answer here.

PRACTICE TEST

Number	Answer	Category	Explanation
96	B	IV.	The skills listed in the question are functional skills. Therefore, the SFA is the best assessment for this situation. The SFA addresses not only classroom access but also playground, lunch, physical education, and other school areas.
97	A	V.	All of the answers are part of IDEA's 6 principles. However, procedural safeguards, Principle 6, ensure that the rights of children with disabilities and their parents are protected and that they have access to the information needed to effectively participate in the process.
98	D	V.	Section 504 regulations require a school district to provide a free appropriate public education (FAPE) to each qualified student with a disability who is in the school district's jurisdiction, regardless of the nature or severity of the disability.
99	B	V.	Measurable goals are required by law under Principle 3 of IDEA.
100	B	V.	Contact information is most important in this situation. All teachers should have parent contact information.
101	D	V.	Procedural safeguards in IDEA are all about parent rights and involvement. Whenever a change is made to an IEP or services of any kind, parents must be notified.
102	D	V.	The Individuals with Disabilities Education Act or IDEA is a federal law that makes available a free appropriate public education (FAPE) to eligible children with disabilities throughout the nation and ensures special education and related services to those children.
103	C	V.	State benchmarks are standards. Therefore, an IEP that has goals focused on benchmarks in the curriculum is standards-based.
104	C	V.	Students are eligible for services under IDEA from the ages of 3-21.
105	A	V.	Parents have a variety of procedural protections they can invoke when they disagree with educators or decisions made on behalf of their children. A due process hearing is the most common.
106	Boxes 1, 2 & 3	V.	Formative assessment is constantly happening in the classroom through observations and informal check, and, therefore, does not need parental approval. However, all the other circumstances listed do.
107	B	V.	While all the disabilities listed qualify someone for special education services, the only disability listed in the answer choices that is part of the 13 disabilities outlined in IDEA is visual impairment. ADHD falls under other health impairment. Cerebral palsy falls under orthopedic impairment. Down Syndrome falls under intellectual disability.

Praxis Special Education

Number	Answer	Category	Explanation
108	B	V.	IDEA is the Individuals with Disabilities Education Act and is a Federal law enacted in 1975. FAPE is Free and Appropriate Public Education, LRE is Least Restrictive Environment, and FERPA is Family Educational Rights and Privacy Act.
109	D	V.	Children with disabilities have the right to receive their education in the school and the classroom they would attend if they were not disabled. However, some students need special classes or services. The goal is to keep special education students included in the general curriculum. The least restrictive environment in this question is the general classroom. The second least is participating in culinary and then going back into a special education classroom. Finally, the most restrictive environment is the self-contained classroom.
110	D	V.	Procedural safeguards are rules and procedures that must be used when making decisions about a student's special education services. A parent teacher conference on academics does not apply.
111	A	V.	Parents and students have the right, under the law, to be actively involved with the IEP process and decisions made by the IEP team. A teacher should NEVER make changes to an IEP. Rather, she should share observations and data during the IEP meeting, so the team can make decisions collectively. The team includes the parents and the student.
112	D	V.	Under Free Appropriate Public Education (FAPE), students who live in the United States, who are at least three years old and less than 22 years old, who meet the eligibility criteria, and who have not yet graduated from high school with a standard diploma, are entitled to receive free special education services from the local school district.
113	D	V.	Under the Family Education Rights and Privacy Act (FERPA), student records are protected and only the parents or legal guardians of students should get access to student records. The request should be refused on the grounds of FERPA.
114	A	V.	Cultural bias often contributes to students being mislabeled and English language learners (ELL) can often end up in special education classes. It is very important that teachers and administrators examine their cultural bias when classifying ELL students as special education.
115	B	V.	Parents should be actively involved in the IEP process and need to understand everything going on the IEP meeting. If parents do not speak English, the school must provide proper accommodations so the parents can understand what is happening in the meetings. This is the right of the parents, which is protected under the federal law, IDEA.

Number	Answer	Category	Explanation
116	A	V.	Accommodations, goals/objectives, and least restrictive environment are all part of the IEP. Peer-interaction data is not.
117	A	V.	The PLAAFP is a key part of the Individualized Education Program (IEP). The very first PLAAFP for students describes students' skills and abilities based on his initial special education evaluation.
118	C	V.	The question tests understanding of the referral and identification process. Before a student can be recommended for placement for special education services, there must be evidence showing that a response to intervention (RTI) has been implemented and documented. Sometimes this is referred to as MTSS.
119	D	V.	The only requirement under IDEA listed in the answer choices is LRE. If you see LRE in an answer choice, slow down and consider it because it is most likely the answer on a special education test.
120	B	V.	Transition planning begins at age 14. This is when students modify their goals to postsecondary goals. The IEP team determines what is the best course of action for life after high school.

PRACTICE TEST

Bibliography

Center for Disease Control (2018). 1 in 4 US adults live with a disability: Cognitive disability most common in younger adults; mobility disability most common for others. Retrieved from https://www.cdc.gov/media/releases/2018/p0816-disability.html

DiPasquale, G. (n.d.). Comorbidity: Learning Disabilities Association of Ontario. Retrieved from https://www.ldao.ca/introduction-to-ldsadhd/articles/about-lds/considering-coexisting-conditions-or-comorbidity-2/

Federal Interagency Forum on Child and Family Statistics. (2009). *America's children: Key national indicators of well-being*. Washington, D.C.: U.S. Government Printing Office.

Georgia Department of Education (2011). Special Education Supplement Glossary. Retrieved from https://www.gadoe.org/Curriculum-Instruction-and-Assessment/Special-Education-Services/Documents/Supplement%20-%20Glossary.pdf

Gordillo, W., (2015). Top 10 trends in special education. Retrieved from https://www.scilearn.com/blog/2015-special-education-trends

Hansen S, Lignugaris/Kraft B. Effects of a dependent group contingency on the verbal interactions of middle school student with emotional disturbance. Behavioral Disorders. 2005;30:169–184.

Harry, B., Klinger, J.K., Sturges, K.M., & Moore, R. (2002). Of rocks and soft places: Using qualitative methods to investigate disproportionality. In D. J. Losen, & G. Orfi eld (Eds.), Racial inequity in special education. Cambridge, MA: Harvard Education Press.

Hurst, S. (2014). What's the difference between RTI and MTSS? Reading Horizons. Retrieved from https://www.readinghorizons.com/blog/what-is-the-difference-between-rti-and-mtss

IDEA Partnership (n.d.) Functional behavior assessment. Retrieved from http://www.ideapartnership.org/documents/ASD-Collection/asd-dg_Brief_FBA.pdf

Long, E. J., Long, J. N., & Whitson, S. (2009). The angry smile: the psychology of passive aggressive behavior in families, schools and workplaces (2nd ed.). Austin: PRO.ED, Inc.

National Research Council. (2002). Minority students in special and gifted education. Committee on Minority Representation in Special Education, M. Suzanne Donovan and Christopher T. Cross, (Eds.) Division of Behavioral and Social Sciences and Education. Washington, DC: National Academy Press.

Rubin, I. L., & Crocker, A. C. (1989). *Developmental disabilities: Delivery of medical care for children and adults*. Philadelphia: Lea & Febiger.

The Center on Positive Behavior Interventions and Supports (PBIS) (n.d.). *Tiered Framework*. Retrieved from https://www.pbis.org/pbis/tiered-framework

The Division on Career Development and Transition of the Council for Exceptional Children (2018). *Appendix A: National secondary transition technical assistance center (NSTTAC) age-appropriate transition assessment article*. Retrieved from https://www.iidc.indiana.edu/styles/iidc/defiles/INSTRC/TransitionAssessment/7%20Transition%20Assessment%20Resource%20Guide%20-%20Appendices%20A%20&%20B.pdf

The Global Educator Institute (2015). *7 critical areas for arranging your special education classroom*. Retrieved from http://geiendorsed.com/blog/learning-environment/7-critical-areas-for-arranging-your-special-education-classroom/

The U.S. Department of Education (2015). Disabilities discrimination: Overview of the laws. Office for Civil Rights. Retrieved from https://www2.ed.gov/about/offices/list/ocr/disabilityoverview.html

The U.S. Department of Education (2021). Every Student Succeeds Act (ESSA). Retrieved from https://www.ed.gov/essa

The U.S. Department of Education (2021). No Child Left Behind (NCLB). Retrieved from https://www.ed.gov/nclb

Made in the USA
Coppell, TX
24 February 2024

29349859R00070